Trampolining—beginner to competitor

Rob Walker

TRAMPOLINING – BEGINNER TO COMPETITOR

A & C Black · London

First published 1983, revised 1985
Published by A & C Black (Publishers) Ltd,
35, Bedford Row, London WC1R 4JH

ISBN 0 7136 5531 3

British Cataloguing in Publication Data
Walker, Rob
Trampolining.
1. Trampolining
I. Title
796.4′7 GV555

Acknowledgements
The author would like to thank the illustrator, J. C. Walker, and Stewart Atkins and Juliette Airey for their assistance with the photographs.

Typeset in 10pt Plantin by The Word Factory,
Rossendale, Lancashire.
Reproduction by Colthouse Repro Ltd.,
Bournemouth, Dorset, England.

Printed and bound in Italy by
Legatoria Editoriale Giovanni Olivotto, Vicenza.

Contents

Introduction

THE SPORT OF TRAMPOLINING

There is a story about the origin of trampolining which has it that the Eskimos used to toss their men up into the air on walrus skins or blankets. We are not told if those tossed into the air then performed somersaults and other moves or if they just came straight back down into the blanket or walrus skin.

In the 1920s and 1930s there were a number of acts in music halls and circuses in which a 'bouncing bed' was the main item of equipment. These beds were often covered with simulated bedclothes to hide the frame and springs, so that it looked as if the act was being performed on a real bed. There are still circus acts which use the trampoline but, while some are very entertaining, in most cases the level of skill is not high.

George Nissen, a US tumbling and diving champion, was the person who developed the equipment and started the sport as we know it today. He built his own gear and used it for personal fun and for the training and entertainment of others during and after the Second World War. After the war the first competitions were held, in the USA, and the development of competitive trampolining had begun.

In Britain a number of people had built their own trampolines: some were gymnasts, some divers. Ted Blake was one. He built a trampoline at Loxford School, in Ilford, and later was instrumental in developing the sport throughout Britain and Europe.

The first competitions were held in the late 1950s. In Britain the Amateur Gymnastic Association took initial responsibility for the sport and staged a number of championships. The first champions, Brian Phelps and Margaret Austen, were both divers.

The first association in Britain formed solely to promote trampolining was the Scottish Trampoline Association, and the British Trampoline Association followed, in England. The British Trampoline Federation was formed in 1964 from the amalgamation of the Amateur Gymnastic Association Trampoline Committee and the British Trampoline Association. In England, Wales and Northern Ireland the sport is today administered by the BTF, the Welsh and Irish bodies having become affiliated comparatively recently.

The sport of trampolining has developed very rapidly, and the moves displayed have advanced from the simple somersault to, for example, triple-twisting double somersaults. Trampolining is characterised by the amount of time spent in the air and by the variety of landing and take-off positions it is possible to use—namely on the feet, bottom, stomach and back. The top performers reach a height of over 7.5m (about 25ft) from the floor, which means that they travel a distance through the air of some 15m (50ft), since the very high jumper almost reaches the floor at the bottom of the stretch of the bed on landing. By comparison, a diver from the 10m (33ft) board travels a distance of only 10m and in only one direction, downwards. The trampolinist therefore spends much longer in the air and has much more freedom of expression as he or she travels 7.5m upwards, slows to a point of weightlessness, and then drops 7.5m back down again onto the bed. Even a novice can easily jump more than a metre vertically, giving a flight of nearly 3m (10ft), since the bed is depressed a bit as the trampolinist lands.

TYPES OF TRAMPOLINE

There are three principal sizes of trampoline in use at the present: the Junior, the 77a and the Goliath. In addition, there is a special competition trampoline for limited high-level performance, the Dinamic. All are manufactured by Nissen International, the main trampoline manufacturer in Britain. The overall frame size of the Junior is 360cm x 210cm x 81cm (12ft x 7ft x 2ft 8in). The frame size of the 77a is 460cm x 274cm (15ft x 9ft) and that of the Goliath 510cm x 304cm (16ft 9in x 10ft). The Dinamic is a specially produced trampoline, the frame of which is 5.2 metres long, 3 metres wide and 1.15 metres high. Special end frames, padded for safety in case a performer lands outside the frame, effectively increase the dimensions. These trampolines, or others with the same specifications, are mandatory for international competitions.

Trampoline beds are made from nylon: they can take the form of a solid sheet, a 1¾in (44mm) web, a 1in (25mm) web, a ½in (12mm) web or, for top-level competition and performance, a ¼in (6mm) web. The last two sizes are known also as 12mm and 6mm beds.

For general use and for maximum effective life time, the solid and the 1¾in beds are recommended. For reasonably good performance and long life, the 1in bed is very good value. For high performance, the 12mm and 6mm beds are necessary—and there is a considerable difference in their performances. A club with competition as its main aim should be prepared to invest in an expensive trampoline like the Dinamic.

The main reason for the difference in performance of the various types of bed is air resistance. The solid bed is like a sail: it has to displace a large volume of air when it is put in motion. The webbed bed, by contrast, lets much of the air pass through its holes. The thinner the gauge of the nylon strip used, the more air can pass through, so that the bed can be depressed more easily and will return more swiftly to the 'rest' position after depression.

String beds are popular in Australia and are becoming so in the USA. These are very fast, since the amount of air able to pass through is far greater than with the nylon-web beds. They do not tend to be quite as stable as the nylon-web beds, but they are gradually being improved; they are, of course, very long-lasting and easily maintained. Very few are in use in Europe, although they can be made to the specifications demanded by the international rules.

One thing is certain about beds: users have very different ideas on which bed is best for them. Their selection is determined by experience, need, fashion and cost. Consulting the manufacturer can help you choose the bed best suited to your needs and your pocket.

BASIC SAFETY

Any activity where there is movement or projection through the air is potentially dangerous—particularly in the case of a bad landing or one made on a hard metal area or piece of projecting metal. The trampoline allows you to move a considerable distance through the air, to land on your seat, feet, front or back, and to somersault and twist; but there is the risk of being projected over the side of the trampoline onto the hard floor, landing on the metal surrounding the bed, or falling through the springs. It is, therefore, sensible to take precautions before, during and after the activity.

The equipment is heavy, and anyone using it (other than small children) ought to learn how to fold and unfold it under supervision without risking injury. If necessary, the folding and unfolding should be carried out by trained staff. The latest competition trampolines have special instructions attached to the frame, and these should be strictly adhered to when erecting and putting the equipment away.

The trampoline should be kept locked or stored away in a locked room when not in use.

Equipment check

It is important to know what to check on the equipment so that you may carry out a simple remedy or, if need be, report the fault for correction by the manufacturer or serviceman. Checks should be carried out frequently: some problems are obvious but others need to be specially looked for. Check

- ☐ on older models, the Allen Screws at the top of the leg braces and where the chains are attached
- ☐ on later models, the wire strainers on the chains
- ☐ the hinges on the frame (bowing of the top indicates wear on the hinges)
- ☐ the anchor bars (for wear from the hooks of the springs or cables)
- ☐ the frame pads (for soft spots or missing clips)
- ☐ the springs or cables (to see that the hooks all point downwards)
- ☐ the beds (for wear of the stitches and the webbing or sheet nylon); check also the nylon anchor bars for wear
- ☐ for high tension in the bed, caused by shrinkage (extenders are available to remedy this)
- ☐ for uneven centre lines, caused by uneven tensions of the springs on opposite sides of the bed (move springs or cables to remedy this)
- ☐ that roller stands are well away from the trampoline, so that no one can fall over or onto them

Safety considerations

- ☐ The trampoline should be well away from any projections which could cause injury and from overhead obstructions. It should be sited in an area with at least 5.5m (18ft) clear for ordinary use and 7-7.5m (23-25ft) for top-level competition and training.
- ☐ When folding the trampoline, *never* pull the frame towards you. There is a chance that it could fall on you if the wheels are checked by an unevenness of the floor or ground.
- ☐ *Never* allow the trampoline frame to be left open with the leg braces released unless it is held down by a responsible person. The bed is under considerable tension, and the end frame will fly up if lifted even a few centimetres unless under restraint. *Serious injury could occur if this were allowed to happen.*

1. *Allen Screws*
2. *Hinges*
3. *Chains and wire strainers*
4. *Leg braces*
5. *Roller stands*
7. *Pads*
8. *Springs/cables/hooks/anchor bars*
9. *Bed/strands*

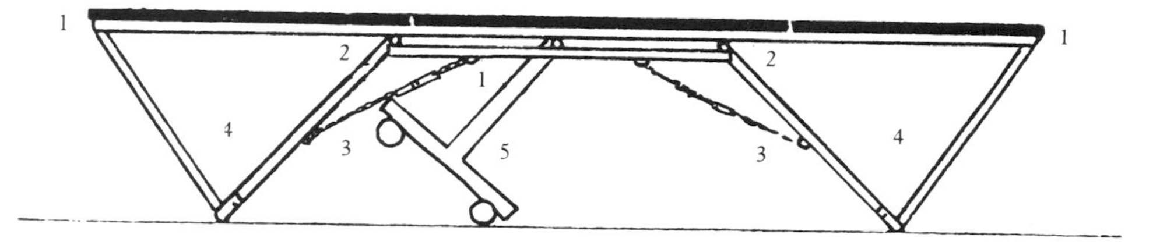

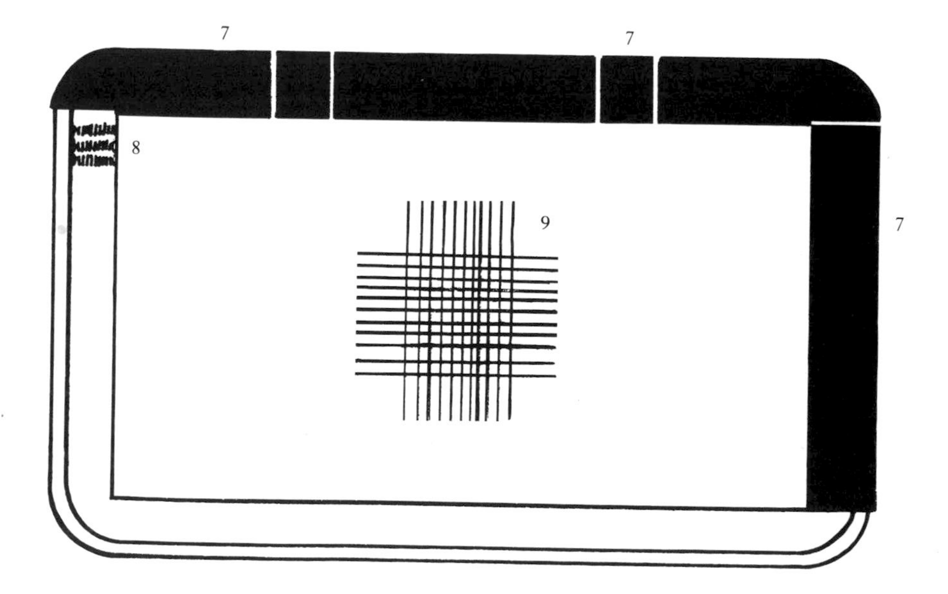

The BTF strongly recommends that anyone wishing to teach trampolining should hold an appropriate award. These awards are graded through from the lowest level to the most advanced. They cover all requirements for teaching all moves at the various levels of skill involved in the sport. Most local authorities require teachers to hold a coaching award; the level is set by the authority. The BTF recommends that the Coach Award is the minimum level for those who wish to teach up to somersaults. The more advanced awards, covering intermediate and advanced skills, are aimed at those who wish to teach the sport to competition level. Courses are run by the BTF at all levels over the whole of Britain (see page 95).

This safety check-list will help even the most highly qualified coach keep in mind the major safety considerations.

☐ trampolining should take place under the supervision of a qualified coach
☐ short turns (45 seconds to one minute) are best for all levels of skill
☐ no double-bouncing without permission
☐ no horseplay
☐ no chewing gum or eating on the trampoline
☐ no jewellery, watches or rings, or articles which could catch on the bed or could harm a spotter or the performer
☐ no participation without the appropriate clothing
☐ no jumping without at least four spotters (crash mats at the ends of the trampoline can be used as an alternative to two of the spotters)
☐ pupils should not attempt new skills without using progressions or without your checking their readiness for the next level
☐ no somersaulting without permission
☐ do not use the rig without first checking the ropes, shackles and buckles and the weight of the pupil
☐ do not allow any first attempts at advanced-level single-somersault skills or multiple somersaults without the use of the rig or a crash mat, or both
☐ report any accident: your immediate report of the circumstances could be important both for you and for the trainee

Here is a safety check-list for learners.

- ☐ never attempt to unfold or fold the trampoline on your own or if the person in charge is not present
- ☐ never work-out alone
- ☐ never attempt moves beyond your known ability
- ☐ never get involved in 'tests of daring' with others
- ☐ pay attention to the advice of your coach
- ☐ pay attention at all times when spotting for others
- ☐ if in doubt ASK the coach or supervisor

SAFETY AIDS

There are other aids which can be used to help ensure the safety of the learner at all times, during teaching and practice. Most frequently used is the crash mat, followed by the safety harness or rig.

The crash mat is easy to use: learners can be trained to do so, allowing the coach to concentrate on techniques while the learners trained to use the mat can push it in at the appropriate time.

The rig is better left to the experienced coach or teacher since considerable practice is required before one is able to use the rig to the best advantage of the trainee.

The best safety aid of all is good teaching. If the teaching is good then there is less likelihood of accident—whatever other safety aids are used. Coaches should remember that the learner entrusts them with the task of ensuring that progress is made *with safety*. Coaches have a 'duty of care' to all those being taught. This 'duty of care' is a legal obligation: the consequences of neglecting to take it can be serious not only for the learner but also for the coach.

The crash mat

The crash mat is one of the pieces of equipment which has helped trampolinists perform ever more difficult manoeuvres over the last few years. It has also increased safety when used at the ends of the trampoline, either with or without spotters. As well as being the easiest safety aid to use, it is overall the most effective—it can be employed at any level from the front drop to the two-and-three-quarter front somersault.

The cost of the equipment is not very high, and learners can handle it for each other; this has the additional benefit of training the members of the group in self-help and in concentration on the work of their fellow members. All those entrusted with pushing in the crash mat for others must practise the proper timing, so that the mat does not get pushed in too soon or too late. Coaches should select for the job some of the older and more responsible group members, and start on simple moves with a spoken count. Something as elementary as the seat drop can be used to start with—somersaults can follow when more experience has been gained.

Moves like the full twist to front drop (see page 36) and half-twist duck under are more easily learned if the crash mat is used to ameliorate the knocks likely to occur during the early stages. Some learners are particularly apprehensive and need the mat in learning even the front drop (see page 31). The mat absorbs the uneven landings so that the learner can concentrate on the take-off without worrying too much about the landing.

For somersaults, the mat is good at absorbing over- or under-rotated landings, and is particularly useful for the transitional stage from the rig to free performance.

The safety harness or rig

Using the rig is a skilful and tiring task. No one should make a first attempt at double somersaults unless supported by the coach in the rig—this is especially important for heavier learners. Even if the coach cannot stop the learner, the descent can be slowed so that the landing is gentle and safe. The rig can be used, too, to help give the learner a small lift and thus more time in the air to complete a move on the descent.

The coach must not let the rig interfere too much with the learner's freedom to move in the air by pulling too hard on the ropes; nor should he

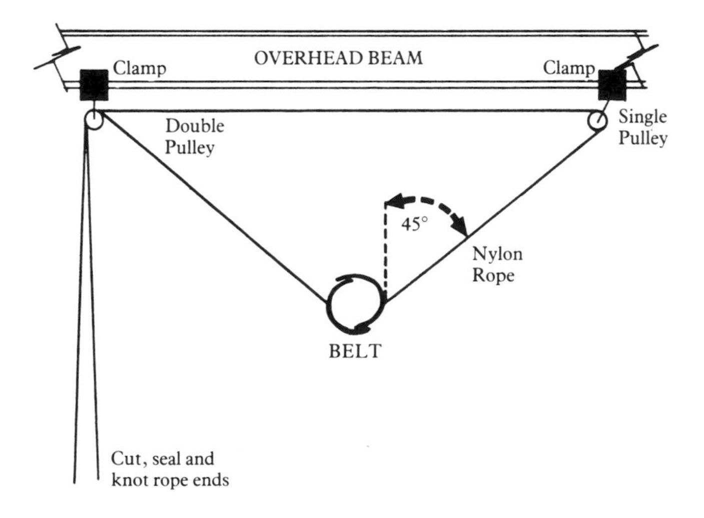

allow too much slack in the ropes and thereby create the risk of the athlete getting tangled up in them. These are very important elements in the skilful use of the rig.

On very advanced skills, like the two-and-three-quarter front somersault, the coach must be able to hold the learner, since the landing is high on the shoulders and has to be well judged. Any error of judgement on the learner's part must, to avoid accident, be covered by the coach.

As the learner becomes more proficient, the coach can let a little slack into the rope for the descent, provided the learner is coming down safely. The coach's decision time for this is very short, and so a good deal of experience is necessary.

Used in conjunction with the crash mat, the rig gives a safety in landing otherwise impossible. Both are essential for those who take trampolining seriously and wish to advance to more difficult moves. The somersaulting belt is adjustable, from large to very small; and the twisting belt comes in two sizes and is adjustable through a reasonable range of waist sizes. Both can be used for front and for back landings. It may be wise to pad the twisting belt around the learner's waist if front or back landings are to be performed; this avoids bruised ribs caused by the hard sides of the belt.

The supporter may need to wear some form of hand protection—either a towel wrapped around the rope or some gardening gloves—to avoid rope burns when a rapidly descending athlete has to be braked swiftly.

The rig should be kept in good condition and inspected regularly.

Kipping

In order to give learners any successful form of support on the trampoline bed, the coach must first learn the art of 'kipping'. This is leg action by the supporter which can avoid killing the bounce of the bed during take-off, add a little more power to the take-off, or help stabilise the level of the learner's jumping. The supporter pushes down on the bed just as the athlete lands, so that the weight of two people is depressing the bed. As the bed rises from its lowest point the supporter quickly bends his legs so that the extra stored energy is transmitted to the other. A practised supporter is able to adjust the amount of energy in accordance with the other's needs. This is necessary since it is almost impossible for a second person to be on the bed without having an effect upon the performance of the bed and therefore of the learner, too.

Before any form of hand supporting is attempted, the coach must become proficient at kipping so that the learner will not lose confidence in the support available. That said, some of the bigger and more able group members should be taught how to kip in case there is a need for support by two persons when the learner is attempting somersaults for the first time.

Hand supports

In the teaching of beginners and intermediates the ability to support by hand is a distinct advantage. The idea is primarily to provide psychological support, as well as physical support if necessary. The supporter should be competent, supporting the performance rather than interfering with it. He or she may use the learner's clothing, body or hands as a gripping surface, or may wrap a towel or judo belt around the learner's waist. Whatever the method used, the supporter must be able (a) to exert a good lift and turning force, and (b) to slow down and direct the learner's landing.

Almost all the basic moves can be hand supported. Initially, the supporter must stand close to the learner with a good grip on him or her; then move away to allow the learner to start alone; and then finally move in again after take-off to support the landing.

Clearly the supporter has to be a skilled kipper and have good eye and hand coordination to be able to take a firm hold on learners in mid-flight and bring them in to a good landing. A good supporter can improve the learning rate of the trainee to a considerable extent. Any failure on the supporter's part leads to the learner losing confidence in both himself and the supporter.

Hand supports can be used in conjunction with the crash mat to give even easier landing for the learner, so that he or she can concentrate on the technical skill of a move rather than worry about the pain of the landing or the fright of the flight. The supporter must practise these skills by starting with the simple moves before going on to the more complex ones.

Spotting decks

For competition training and performance there are high performance trampolines which are a little larger and higher from the floor than the standard large trampoline. Also available for extra safety are *spotting decks* which are frames easily attached to the ends of the trampoline. These frames are sprung and have crash mats fitted on them to absorb the heaviest landings by a performer. They are much more secure than the crash mat resting on a beam or box, but they are more expensive. For the serious competitive club, however, they are well worth the expense.

1
Starting skills

JUMPING AND STOPPING

The primary skill on the trampoline is jumping: although performed more than any other it is, however, often done poorly. This may be because learners are allowed to jump with little or no instruction. A small amount of effort early on will pay enormous dividends.

The legs are pushed down into the trampoline and then extended fully before they leave the bed. The toes, the last part of the foot to leave the bed, should also be fully extended. The extension must be strong, and held as the body rises up into the air. The spine must be straightened by turning the tail under a little and the head must be held in line, tilted neither up nor down. Any movement of the head, either forward or backward, will result in the body piking or arching a little in flight. The eyes can look ahead in flight, but should pick up the bed before the final part of the descent is made. The whole action should be smooth and powerful, not jerky.

To stop, the legs should bend quickly on the last contact so that the bed is not depressed too much—very little energy will then be stored in it, and there will be very little rebound to deal with, making staying in contact with the bed's surface comparatively easy. On the high-powered competition beds, with jumping heights of 7.5m (25ft) or more, it can be very difficult to stop dead under control, but for the average trampolinist on the average trampoline it is relatively easy.

ARM ACTION

An important factor in good jumping is efficient use of the arm swing. Watching trampolinists jump might make you wonder why so many different actions are used. This is largely a result of the various instructions given by those who teach the sport; attempts to correct the results of poor body alignment or movement of the head during the jumping action are another cause. One thing is certain: not all of the actions on display can give efficient performance. Some must be good, some inefficient and thus counterproductive.

The arms are used to help depress the bed, to give upward and rotational momentum, to assist with balance in flight, and to accelerate somersaults and twists. Arm action is obviously, therefore, very important: good use of the arms will improve all aspects of your performance, while poor use will make it more difficult to perform well.

To help depress the bed, the arms must be swung down from behind the trunk at the moment of contact between the feet and the bed. The arms should be straight as they pass through the lowest point of the swing and then begin to move upwards. From this point onwards they can be kept straight, allowed to bend at the elbow, stopped at shoulder height, or lifted up to a near-vertical position: stopping straight arms at about shoulder height will give most upward transfer; swinging them up to a vertical position will lessen the upward transfer but may cause a backward movement of the shoulders; letting the arms bend at the elbow will lessen the transfer in any direction.

The recovery phase of the arm swing should be easy and relaxed, and happen early enough to ensure that no jerky movements, which will adversely affect the body in flight, need to be made. Bending the arms helps ensure less adverse reaction since less effort is needed to move them.

In flight the arms need to be moved about only to aid balance. If by chance the performer is a little off-balance in flight, some movement of the arms will help. If a lot of movement is needed it is probably better to stop jumping and start again.

The arms can assist both lift and rotation. For backward rotation, the arm action should be vigorous and brought to a stop at or just above shoulder level for maximum transfer. Since the arms are moving in an arc there is some backward effect as they are stopped. The main rotation is from the forward displacement of the hips. Notice the difference in the speed of movement of the arms in the single and the double back somersault: in the latter the arms move much faster before being stopped.

For forward rotation, although most of the rotational force is obtained from the backward displacement of the hips, there seem to be two main ways in which the arms are used. In one, the arms are left in the air as the landing is made; they are then aimed upwards and pulled into the tuck after take-off. However, in many cases the performer leaves the arms too far forward, so that there is a downward pull as the take-off is made, resulting in a loss of height. The other is where the arms are lifted upwards in a normal swinging action as take-off is made. Some upward momentum is transferred to the body so that height is not lost. This longer body shape, enhanced by lift, gives improved acceleration.

For twisting, the arms are swung as for a normal jump but extended to the side instead of continuing in a lift. The proper use of the arms is to provide a means of acceleration, not a means of initiating twist. While the feet are still in contact with the bed, the upper body and head are turned in the direction of twist with the arms held firmly out to the side. The degree to which the shoulders are turned and the force with which they are turned

determine the amount of twisting force developed at take-off. Any slackness or lack of sideways reach of the arms lessens the effectiveness of the acceleration when the arms are brought in close to the sides. Of course, the skilled performer soon learns the amount of power and acceleration needed for each particular move. The speed with which the arms are brought in to the sides determines the speed of acceleration. The amount of twisting force and the difference between the width of the arms at the take-off and in the middle of the twist determine the maximum speed of twist.

The arms can either be brought down to the sides of the body or crossed on the chest. Both methods are acceptable, but each has slightly different characteristics both in feel and to the spectator. Coach and trainee will decide for themselves which style they feel is better. Smooth performance and ease of phasing must be sought, whatever type of action is used. Unfortunately, many learners are allowed to consolidate bad performance through continuous practice of poor techniques.

FORWARD AND BACKWARD ROTATION

All rotation is produced by applying eccentric force about an axis. In the case of forward and backward rotation the force is applied about the lateral (side-to-side) axis of the body. The necessary eccentric force is produced by displacing the hips backwards from the vertical (for forward rotation) or forwards (for backward rotation). However, it is the rebound of the bed which provides the propulsive force itself; the hip positioning then converts this into rotational force. This is a very efficient way of producing rotation, avoiding much height loss while still giving a powerful rotation. It is important to use a strong downward push into the bed.

Any forward or backward lean produces rotation, too—in fact, this is the easiest method of rotating. However, it leads to loss of height and to travel (horizontal movement, forward or backward). Some performers start somersaults with their arms high above their heads as they take off. This aims the body upwards, but can also easily lead to travel and loss of height if the arms are allowed to move too far forward or backward. It suffers as a technique from loss of upward momentum from the arms. The wise coach will evaluate various methods of performance to see which are efficient as opposed to merely fashionable.

Assuming there is no lean, very little displacement is needed for single or double somersaults. Too much displacement leads to a dropping of the shoulders either forwards or backwards, and should be avoided when learning somersaults.

From a stomach landing, backward rotation can be produced by kicking the legs downwards or just by ensuring that the lower leg is clear of the bed on impact. The buttocks should be contracted tightly to avoid loss of transfer. Once free of the bed the body can be held tight or, to increase the speed of rotation, tucked up. Thus rotation from front to feet is produced in the same way as in the cody: differing amounts of rotational force are created as required.

Forward rotation from the back

Greater eccentric force can be developed from the back landing than from the front landing: this is because the whole leg length contributes to initiating rotation. Moreover, since the knee and hip joints enable you to vary your direction of thrust, a number of variations in direction can be effected. These will have markedly different effects upon your performance.

Somersaults should normally have height and be without cast (sideways horizontal movement) or travel. If the legs are kept straight on landing they can rotate only about the hip joint, and normally will do so in a forward and downward direction. People with great flexibility about the hip joint and long hamstring muscles can bring their legs well up towards the trunk, so that the first phase of the leg action is upwards, exerting a

downward push, but very little eccentric force, on the bed. As they pass through the vertical, still rotating forwards, greater eccentric force develops, and this is transferred when the hips are locked.

Those who are less supple will have difficulty executing the move. Instead, they should land with the legs projecting past the end of the trunk, bent at the knees and held under considerable tension; this gives height and generates considerable rotational force, without travel. With practice a performer can set the legs in the best position. Height can be increased by a more powerful upward kick from the lower leg; and greater tension in the stomach and hip flexor muscles when holding the legs in place will contribute to greater rotational efficiency.

This starting position also allows good transfer of rotational momentum, since the body is not held in too straight and long a position as the take-off is started, and the stomach does not have to be as strong to hold the body position.

TWISTING

The initiation of twisting force requires another application of eccentric force about an axis, this time about the body's longitudinal axis.

As we have seen (see page 17), good arm action is integral to good twisting. However, the twisting force is best generated by the strong muscles of the trunk, the external oblique muscles. It can be generated from a front, back or standing take-off and in mid-air: the principle is the same although the effect looks different in each position. In all situations, except in mid-air, part of the body is fixed on the bed while the shoulders turn. In mid-air one part of the body provides a resistance against which the other part can turn; the resistance is then lessened by altering the shape of the body.

From the feet

While the feet are in contact with the bed during the jumping action the shoulders are turned in the direction of desired twist by the main action of the trunk muscles. This must be carried out without lean or dropping of the shoulders which will result in travel, cast, or both, as well as loss of height. As stated before (see page 20) the arms provide a means of acceleration after the twist has been set up. Thus, while the trunk generates twist, the arms should be held rigid in some position such that they are as one with the trunk until you want to accelerate the speed of twist. This applies in forward, backward and vertical twisting. Any sloppiness of your arms or trunk will lessen the efficiency of the movement.

From the back

When twisting from a back landing, the twist is still produced by turning your shoulders in the direction of twist. As soon as contact is made with the bed the shoulders are turned: one shoulder lifts but the other is stopped from moving backwards by the pressure of the bed. As soon as the body clears the bed both shoulders rotate. Efficiency depends upon the timing of the twist, the tension in your body and the use of your arms to accelerate.

From the front

Because landing on the front requires the arms for support, you must use your arms to set up twist from the landing position. To twist to your right, push your left arm down into the bed as your body leaves the bed; obviously, the right arm must not simultaneously push down. It is more difficult to set up a powerful twisting action from the front than from the back owing to the difference in the flexibility of the body in the two landing positions. As in the twist from the back landing, the body must be kept taut so that all possible twisting force is transferred.

Mid-air twisting

Mid-air twisting—called 'relative moment of inertia twisting' by trampolinists—is dependent upon the body somersaulting to develop enough rotation for multiple twists. On a plain jump it is difficult to achieve much more than a half-twist.

The body must be tucked, piked, pucked or arched. In any of these positions the moment of inertia of the body below the hips is greater than that across the shoulders. Thus it is possible to turn the shoulders to the left or right against the moment of inertia or the resistance of the lower

body to sideways movement. As the body is straightened and the lower body brought into line with the upper, the twisting momentum of the upper body is transferred to the lower so that the whole body twists in the same direction as the shoulders. Folding the body increases the resistance of the lower half and arrests the twist.

This works most efficiently from the piked position and least effectively from the arched position. Even from the latter, it is relatively easy to produce a good full twist.

Twisting and rotating

It is possible for a trampolinist to twist at the same time as somersaulting. While the feet are in contact with the bed and somersault rotation is being initiated by displacement of the hips, it is easy to turn the shoulders at the same time so that rotation about the longitudinal axis is initiated. The body then rises into the air simultaneously somersaulting and twisting. This technique is used for simple stunts like the half-twist as well as for thc front or back drop, full-twisting front and back somersaults and double-twisting double somersaults. Some twisting double somersaults—normally those with the twists in the second somersault only—are performed using the mid-air twisting techniques described above.

BASIC SKILLS

Tuck jump

The easiest move on the trampoline. After take-off, swing your arms high and straight above your head, stretching your body from head to toe. At maximum height, pull your arms down to grasp your knees in front of and

close to your chest, one hand on each shin just below the knee. Let go, stretch, and prepare for the landing. Do not let your heels move backwards or try to reach down for your shins in anticipation of the tuck. To develop correct timing, your coach may call out or signal to you when the shape is to be made.

Pike jump

Still easy to do but requiring more physical effort since the legs are straight. At the maximum height, pull your arms and legs together, keeping them straight. Place your hands on your shins or down by your ankles, either grasping or resting as desired. Let go and stretch as before.

Piked straddle jump

At the maximum height of the jump pull your legs and arms together, keeping them straight; however, keep your legs wide apart in the straddle position. Some performers put their hands on the lower leg, others place the arms and hands midway between the legs; both positions are acceptable.

Jump with full twist

Some performers have a little difficulty with this move; sometimes people lose balance just before landing.

Start with simple half-twist jumps: turn your head and shoulders in the desired direction and use a low jump, but make sure that the jumping action for the legs is correct, stretching them fully and pointing the toes. At this stage your arms may be held by the sides since no acceleration is required. The twisting movement is gentle.

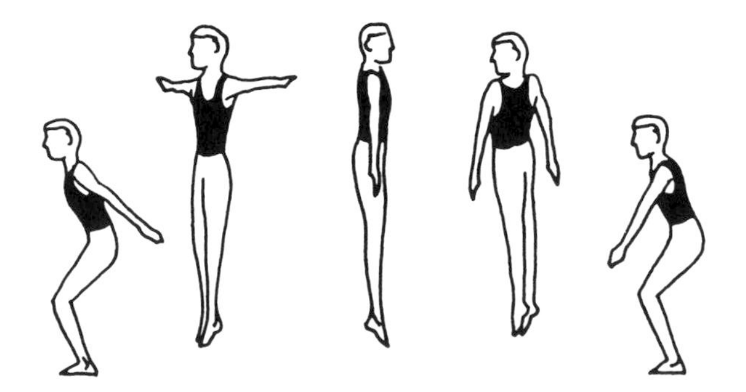

It is good technique to achieve the full twist by use of acceleration rather than by more vigorous twisting action. Initially, hold your arms out to the sides of your body at an angle of about 30-40 degrees, keeping them rigid; turn the head, shoulders and arms as one unit. Practise until you can do this easily and well. Next, take off as before and, after about one-quarter to one-third of a turn, pull your arms in to your sides. This should produce a full twist. If it does not, then turn a little harder or pull your arms in a little earlier.

To accelerate further, hold your arms out at shoulder height and repeat the start and acceleration technique. Then pull your arms down to your sides or cross them on your chest—both techniques are equally effective, but give slightly different performance characteristics.

It is important to bring both arms in to the body at the same time rather than lead with one, which can generate a sideways lean— as can putting too much effort into the turning of your shoulders: after practice the amount of shoulder turn can be judged to a nicety. A steady landing can be achieved by opening your arms wide before the landing and thereby slowing your rate of twist.

Twisting is a much gentler action than it looks. It is highly desirable to phase twists so that it seems as if you jump up, twist, and then stop twisting before landing. This is of course mechanically impossible, but the illusion can be created.

Seat drop

The seat drop is not classified as a rotating move since the trunk does not rotate through 90 degrees. Push your legs down into the bed, swing your arms vertically upwards, and displace your hips very slightly forwards to

give a small amount of rotation about your lateral axis. As your body rises, stretch and let your legs swing gently forwards, folding at the waist as you descend. As your body lands, the whole of your (straight) legs should contact the bed at the same time as your hands are placed on the bed, slightly behind your seat. At this stage, then, your hands, bottom and legs should all be in contact with the bed; your toes should be pointed and your trunk leaning slightly backwards. Push back and down on the bed with your hands. As your body rises it should begin to straighten at the waist. Make sure that your legs are kept straight until just before the landing.

Very little height is needed for this move. It is important that your legs are kept straight throughout except for the landing on the feet. The drop should not be performed by leaning back or by lifting the legs up in front of the body. It can be repeated in swing-time (one after another) without requiring very much height, and is thus a suitable introduction to the repetition of simple skills leading to a continuous performance as in a routine.

Half-twist to seat drop

As the basic moves are learned, it is worth learning to twist into and out of them at an early stage. To perform the half-twist to seat drop, swing your arms forwards and upwards and at the same time turn your head and shoulders in the desired direction. As you descend, fold your body at the hips for the seat-drop landing.

Seat drop half-twist to feet

From the seat-drop landing, push your hands back on the bed and then swing them vigorously forwards and up at the same time as you turn your

head and shoulders in the desired direction. As your body rises and straightens the half-twist will take place. A vigorous arm swing is the key to this move.

Seat drop half-twist to seat drop (the swivel hips)

To perform the swivel hips, push your arms back hard on the bed and swing them forwards and upwards even more vigorously as you turn your shoulders. If you have generated the right amount of forward movement of your body, it will move through a small arc so that a second seat-drop landing will be easy. If you have not created any forward rotation it will be hard to complete the move to seat.

In the learning stages it often helps to progress as follows. Do a half-twist to a seat drop followed by a half-twist up to your feet, and then repeat the sequence. As you get better at this you should find it quite easy just to let the whole move happen as one.

A common fault is to try to swing the legs round horizontally for the half-twist. This makes the move more difficult, since the outstretched legs create a strong resistance to lateral rotation. A strong throw of the arms helps straighten the body and so makes the twist easier. Repetition of this move is a good warm-up practice since it is quite a vigorous movement.

Seat drop full twist to seat drop (roller)

Two methods may be used for this move. In the first you push down into the bed with one hand to produce rotation; in the other you use a turn of the shoulders with the arms held out to the side so that twist can be accelerated.

For the first method, go into a seat drop and push the hips up so that the body is straight and at a low angle to the bed (this can be repeated in swing-time until you get the idea). Return to the seat-drop landing position and push down with one hand, raising the body on that side, to practise the twisting action. To complete the whole move, go into the

seat-drop landing, push the hips up and at the same time push down on one hand to rotate the body away from the pushing hand. As your body rises from the bed, keep pushing with the one hand so that it goes behind your back while the non-pushing hand comes across the front of your body. Try to keep your body straight until a full twist is completed: any bending makes it less likely that the twist will be completed by the time you land. A lean to the side will tend to make you try to stop the rotation.

For the second method, drop into the seat-drop position from a low start, with your arms held out sideways. Practise this a few times from a low position to avoid straining your back, which is unsupported by your arms. Continue by raising your hips until your body is in a straight line at

about the same angle to the bed as in the previous method. Sit on the bed and practise turning your shoulders with your arms held straight and then pulling them in to the chest. Then try the whole movement.

Drop onto your seat with your arms held out sideways, lift your hips at the same time as you turn your shoulders, and then wrap your arms in to your chest: the twist should accelerate rapidly. This works more easily than the first method since it is easier to generate rotational force this way than by pushing down into the bed with your hand. Most learners are surprised at how easy it is to perform this move.

Full twist to seat drop from feet

A delicate move well worth learning to promote good twisting technique. The take-off is at the same angle as for the seat drop (see page 27). Initiate the twist very gently, making sure that the bed is kept in view as you take off—too strong a start to the twist can throw you to one side as well as cause a problem with the positioning of your arms and hands on landing.

Many performers when learning this move drop the leading shoulder and swing the opposite arm too hard. This makes the shoulder drop back and the arm swing across too far, with the net result that you travel backwards and cast to one side. The landing will be extra hard on one hand, and the rebound will again be to the side.

Look down at the bed near your feet and try to keep your gaze fixed on or about this area during the take-off and flight. Keep your feet in line with the centre of the bed.

Front drop

The front drop can be regarded as one-quarter of a front somersault, and the techniques learned for it can be applied directly to the learning of the front somersault (see page 48). It can be performed in the tucked, piked and straight positions.

First lie down on the trampoline bed (or floor) in the correct landing position, face downwards. Raise your arms so that your hands are at about face level and your forearms in contact with the bed; your head should be

raised a little and your body, from chest to knee, should be in contact with the bed. Make sure you can feel the correct angle of your lower leg—about 45 degrees. Practise contracting your buttocks and kicking down your lower legs towards the bed but stopping just before they reach it. This is the mechanism for coming up to your feet after landing.

From the hands-and-knees position, push down on your feet and take off, moving slightly backwards with the hands still in contact to land in the position described above. Rebound back to the hands-and-knees position and repeat. Make sure that you are jumping backwards, not forwards, and are not lifting your seat and legs too high on take-off.

From a low crouch, push your legs down into the bed and take them backwards to drop in the landing position. Make sure that you do not start the movement by leaning forwards and thereby initiating a dive. As you take off, straighten your body out for the landing—no further tucking or piking is necessary.

From a position standing on one leg with the other leg out behind you and your upper body near to horizontal, push down on the standing leg and raise it up beside the other. Your body will then drop down onto the bed for the landing. This progression is useful if you have a persistent habit of leaning forwards.

As soon as you land, kick your legs down sharply towards the bed but stop before contact is made. Contract your buttocks strongly so that your body is held taut and the momentum in your legs is transferred to the rest of your body, which should rotate back up to the standing position. If the buttocks are allowed to relax, you can still get back to your feet, but your upper body will not rotate and it will be difficult for you to learn the front drop to back drop. The push of your arms assists the rotation to feet but is not the main rotating force.

To perform the *tucked front drop*, take off with slightly less rotation than for the straight front drop. Get to the straight position and then tuck. After you have shown a good tucked position, open out for the standard landing.

For the *piked front drop*, again use slightly less rotation. Perform the pike after you have shown the straight position rather than allow a gradual creeping into the piked position immediately after take-off. This is a difficult move to perfect but does help you learn control in the air.

On all forward take-offs avoid excessive hip displacement, which leads to dropping of the shoulders and loss of height. On take-off an upward lift of your arms helps avoid the shoulders dropping.

Half-twist to front drop

The first stage in learning the back somersault with full twist, this move can be approached initially by turning the head and shoulders around to look at the bed behind you or close to your heels, taking off, and continuing the twist to land in the hands-and-knees drop, then dropping to a front-drop landing. Progress is made by working gradually towards a starting position facing straight forward, followed by turning your head and shoulders just as you take off. You should be looking at the bed the

whole time, so that there is no need to refocus on it for the landing. Even though you land on your stomach, the take-off is of the back-drop type, with your legs being pushed forwards.

Half-twist to back drop

This is a very important basic skill since it is a forward twisting move and is the first we have encountered where the vision is kept on the bed as the body turns away from the bed—i.e., for a part of the twist the head is turning in the opposite direction to the shoulders.

A very easy progression is from the hands-and-knees drop. As your body rises clear of the bed, twist your shoulders so that your body completes a half-turn and you land on your back. The advantage of this approach is that you are keeping comparatively low: it is often easier to retain your confidence when closer to the bed. The important point is that you should keep your eyes on the bed as you descend, turning your head only just before landing. When you turn your head your gaze is still on the bed, but looking forward and down the sides of your trunk.

You can then progress to a crouched start—still low and in a balanced position. Push down into the bed with your feet and, as your body lifts, turn your shoulders, keeping your eyes on the bed; then extend your legs to the rear and drop onto your back. Avoid turning your head with your shoulders or swinging your legs round to the side.

As you gain proficiency at a low height, gradually increase the height of the take-off jump. Performed well, this move is very graceful.

Full twist to front drop

This is quite difficult for the beginner but is nevertheless important. The main problem lies in the difficulty of maintaining visual contact with the bed during flight. The half-twist to back drop (see page 35) and the half-twist to front drop (see page 34) are the two progressions needed since this move is a compound of the two. It is usually necessary to use the crash mat during your first attempts at this skill, since even a slightly inaccurate landing can be quite uncomfortable.

From a low starting position, rehearse the half-twist to back drop and the half-twist to front drop, aiming especially for a smooth and sighted start on the half-twist to back drop. Then add a small amount of extra turn, past the back-drop landing position. Move on again by adding an

extra turn of the head in the direction of twist. Practise this at first without a crash mat until you feel it is not too difficult to get as far as a three-quarter twist.

Using a crash mat, which will save you from the painful consequences of an inaccurate landing, repeat the above, but now give yourself a little more height and increase the amount of twist at the start—although you should take care not to rush yourself. Concentrate on holding your gaze on the mat at the start until you have executed at least a quarter of a full twist; then turn your head quickly to relocate your vision on the mat as you come in to land. The higher the jump, the easier it is to keep the mat in sight. Do not remove the crash mat until you are making consistently comfortable landings.

Back drop

Start with the landing position on the back, with your knees bent and your head either in contact with the bed or held clear and forward. The legs can be held straight if you like.

From a very low starting position, perform the flat back landing to

ensure that you are moving your legs forward, rather than dropping your shoulders back, to create rotation. Next, by pushing your legs into the air to create lift, bounce on your back until you have had plenty of practice at landing on it under control. From a crouch take a small jump and move the legs forwards so that you land on the bed with your waist contacting it at the point where your feet were. Land with your legs bent, stomach muscles tense and head held firmly; look at the bed to either side of your

body in order to help hold your head firmly. Some people are able to land with their heads in contact, supported by the bed itself. Work at this until your landing is consistent and comfortable before increasing the height of the jump.

To return to your feet, body tension is necessary if your legs are to create the rotation needed—see page 22.

The back drop, too, may also be performed in the tucked and piked positions.

The back drop with tuck needs a take-off with less rotational force than the straight version—you should take off slightly more vertically. After take-off, bring your knees in to your chest and hold momentarily; then

open them out for the landing. As you gain height with practice, you will be able to open out completely to a straight position before preparing for the landing, but in the early days this will not be possible.

The back drop with pike requires a similar take-off, but a little more rotational speed is a good thing, since the piked position does not speed up the rotation as much as does the tucked. After take-off, fold your body

sharply and reach your hands to your lower leg to touch your toes or shins. As above, it may not be possible for you at first to return to the completely straight body position before landing, but increased height will make this possible.

The tucked and piked shapes on the basic moves give you an opportunity to practise phasing of the different parts of the move—so important for good performance. A wise coach will ensure that you are practised in the variant forms of each move.

Full twist to back drop from feet

Progressions for this move are the half-twist to front drop from feet and the half-twist to back drop from feet in that order. As should be done for the first stage of the half-twist to front drop from feet, start with your feet one-eighth to one-quarter of a turn to the rear. Turn your head and shoulders even further round and focus on the bed. From this position, take off and perform a half-twist to a back drop, so that the top of your body moves less twisting distance than do your feet. Gradually start the twists nearer to the front-facing position as you become more proficient. Make sure that the thrust is upwards, not down and back towards the bed. When you are facing the front, your arms should be swung upwards into a wide-arm position so that the twist can be accelerated in flight. This again is a gentle twist—any excess power can lead to cast and travel.

The twist is decelerated when you fold your body to land on your back. You can make a normal return to your feet or you can perform a full twist to your feet—a nice combination for the tyro twister.

Back drop half-twist to feet

Start by bouncing on your back and rolling over for a stomach landing. Make sure that your feet are held up so that your body is bent at an angle of about 30 degrees as you start the twist. This will give some practice in the technique of twisting from a back landing. To progress further, drop onto your back from your feet and initiate rotation to feet with a twist using the technique given on page 23. The rotation back up to your feet is the same skill as the back drop to feet without twist.

Front drop half-twist to feet

Lie on the bed and go over the technique for twisting from the front landing position. Practise the front drop to feet. Then, with a good landing on the stomach and with your body held very taut, push with one hand to initiate the twist. Avoid raising your seat to get to your feet since this spoils the twisting technique.

Back drop full twist to feet

Practise the back drop half-twist to feet (see above), keeping the arms held rigidly and in line with the shoulders. After take-off, make no further effort to increase the rotation force—this should all be generated while your back is in contact with the bed. The full twist should be achieved by the technique of pulling the arms in to the body so that the twist is

accelerated, as in the jump with full twist. Many performers make the mistake of struggling to get further round by wriggling instead of by accelerating whatever twist they have already put in. Your arms should be brought in to your body after about one third of the full twist has been completed. Keep your body straight to help twist.

Front drop full twist to feet

This move is an extension of the front drop half-twist to feet (see above), with the take-off having more power. The body must be held very taut so that there is very little loss of turning force. In contrast to the half-twist, hold your arms a little wider so that acceleration can be made by pulling them in to the chest well after take-off. The real difficulty in this move is to generate enough turning force from the push on the bed, which is moving

away from the body as the twist is generated. Remember that an equal push by both arms will not generate twist.

Front drop to back drop

This move is a half-somersault from the front landing position to the back landing position. It is a progression for the cody, the latter being a backward one-and-a-quarter somersault from the stomach. The first part is the front drop to feet with a straight body (see page 31). Unless this is mastered, it is difficult to initiate enough rotation to rotate as far as a back-drop landing.

Progress from front drop to feet with a straight body to an immediate back drop. Repeat this until there is a considerable clearance between the feet and the bed for the feet landing. Practise a few tuck jumps to revise the technique for tucking the body; i.e., move the two ends of the body together instead of trying to move only the one end. With a good kick of the lower leg down towards the bed, tightening the buttocks and stopping the kick short of the bed, rise up, holding the body straight; after about one-quarter of the rotation, tuck the body to increase the speed of rotation. It should then be easy to get round to the back.

Frequently this skill is made difficult by letting the buttocks rise up into the air first, which relaxes the tension of the body and prevents the momentum of the lower legs being transferred to the whole body. Another cause of failure is often an anticipation of the tuck, trying to get straight into it from the bed and thus not completing the kick-down. Finally, some performers try to force the shoulders backwards in order to complete the move; this has more of a slowing-down than an accelerating effect.

Once this move is well controlled the learning of the cody is well within the grasp of anyone (remember it needs support, either manual or in the rig).

Back drop to front drop

The back drop to feet (see page 38) is the important part of this move. Provided this can be performed easily—with a straight body, no travel, and clearance for a drop down to the feet—the learner knows how to initiate enough forward rotation with good body tension to be capable of progressing further.

The next stage is to do a back drop to feet (straight) followed immediately by a front drop. (The leg technique required to rotate to your feet without travelling is described on page 38). When you feel you have performed sufficient repetitions of this combination, you should prepare to try the whole move. At first there may be a tendency to rush the start and not attain a good height, so make sure you give a strong kick with a good amount of upward direction at the beginning to give height. You will then find that you do not need to tuck much to get round to the front-drop landing position.

This move is a direct progression for the back drop forward turnover to back drop (porpoise) and rotating further to feet (the ball out). Do not move ahead to these moves without having attained good height and without a crash mat.

Back drop forward turnover with half-twist to back drop

This move is also called the cradle. To perform it successfully you must be able to execute the back drop to front drop with straight body (see above).

Other progressions are back drop half-twist to feet (see page 40), for an early twist, and half-twist to back drop (see page 35), for the late-twisting version. The cradle with early twist is the more useful of the two varieties, since it allows progression to the back drop forward turnover to back drop with one-and-a-half twists and two-and-a-half twists. The late twist is marginally easier but does not facilitate easy progress to more twists.

Practise your back drop to front drop, keeping your body as straight as possible and getting good clearance and a fast forward lift out of the bed. Practise the back drop half-twist to feet with good body tension and arms held out to the side under control. Drop into the back drop and, with a strong kick upwards and forwards while at the same time turning your shoulders in the desired direction, hold the position in flight so that the

twist carries on throughout the move. At first your main fault is likely to be a lack of strong forward rotation and height, giving you too little time to complete the twist; this is often because a well performed move looks as if it does not require much power, and so if you have been watching more experienced trampolinists you may mistake the amount of power you need. Remember that your body needs to have good tension before you make the first landing on your back.

The late-twisting variety needs similar body tension and leg kick, but there is more time to put in the twist as you descend to the bed for the back landing. You should learn both varieties.

Back drop full twist to back drop (cat twist)

This is one of the twisting skills which is not dangerous but adds to your twisting techniques. All twisting skills contribute to your awareness of your body in different relationships to the bed. It helps train your body/eye coordination separate out position in the air from sensation from visual pattern.

Bounce on your back, extending your legs and trunk upwards at about 30 degrees. Tighten your buttocks and extend your arms sideways. Practise this movement until you can do it under control on the spot.

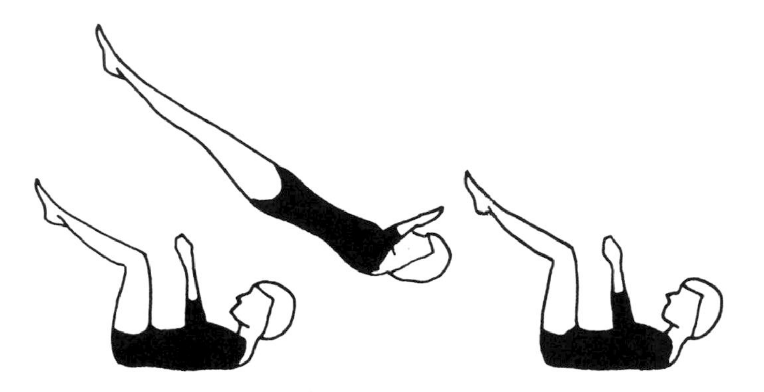

The technique is to turn your shoulders in the desired direction of twist as your back comes into contact with the bed. As you do this, extend your arms sideways from your trunk, ready to pull them in to the body to accelerate the twist after about one-quarter of a twist. Watch the bed as the twist begins, and hold your gaze on the bed until at least three-quarters of a full twist are completed. Make sure your legs are kept high and not dropped down as you rise into the air. Many learners try to throw their arms across their bodies to produce rotation: this does not give a powerful enough rotational force to enable the full twist to be completed easily.

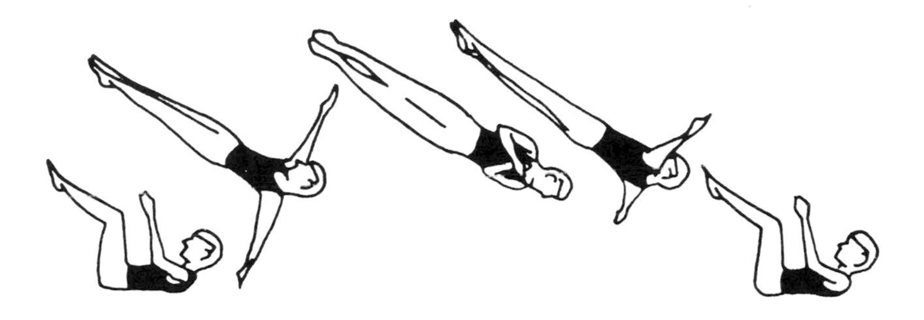

Progress to cat twist, free bounce on the back, cat twist; then try to repeat in swing-time. With more initial turning power and arms held very wide it is possible to go on to double and triple cat twists.

Somersaulting

FRONT SOMERSAULT: SKILLS AND PROGRESSIONS

All somersaulting involves rotating your body by displacing your hips rather than by projecting the top of your body downwards. If you somersault by moving your upper body *down* around your centre of mass, rather than by projecting your lower body *up* around it, your performance and visual awareness will suffer, progress will be limited, and success (if you are a competitive performer) will be less likely however much you train.

Somersaulting necessitates your head being at some time below your body, so rotation must be sufficient to bring your body around to a safe landing position. You must therefore work through a series of progressions, which are individually less likely to cause injury if unsuccessful, and which lead you towards the desired end product—a well performed, safe somersault. Support may often be necessary, as may be the crash mat.

The above applies to both front and back somersaults. Progressions also afford both coach and learner a method of assessing the latter's level of competence.

From hands and knees

The hands-and-knees drop to front drop can be used as the first progression since the leg action is the same (see page 32). Push harder into the bed, so that your body rises higher, move towards the hand-stand position, and then drop back down to the hands-and-knees. This can be performed from a kneeling start rather than a standing one. Make sure that your head is not dropped and your arms not bent in the attempt to create rotation.

Next drop down into the hands-and-knees position and rebound up towards the hand-stand, still keeping your arms straight and your eyes focussed on the bed. Drop back down to hands-and-knees. As soon as you

can create enough rotation by the leg push to lift your body up to the hand-stand regularly, try to turn over onto your back. Again make sure that your arms are not bent nor your head dropped. A slight forward push on your hands as you take off will help prevent forward travel.

Progress to seat landing by tucking your body during flight, opening out to land. A quick tuck should give enough acceleration to allow the seat

landing. Still make sure your head is held up and your arms kept straight for take-off. You are getting practice at tucking while rotating without there being much height to worry about.

From knees

The two progressions above can now be tried from the knee-drop landing. It is easy from this landing to let the head and shoulders drop down, and

you must take care that you do not do this. Make sure your arms are lifted and your body projected upward. Rotation is easy since your feet push into the bed well behind your body—this may lead to travel so, to counteract this, your hips must at this stage be displaced more than for a standing take-off. Progress to tucking in mid-flight to land on your seat. Once again

the object of the progression is to lift as well as rotate. It is now easy to complete a somersault from knees to feet. However, this will tend to be a fast rotation, tightly tucked, and not necessarily the best practice at this stage.

From feet with support

Now that you have practised producing rotation without travel or loss of height and somersault acceleration, you should find it possible, with good support, to complete a standing front somersault with tuck from feet to feet easily.

Two supporters hold your hands or your waist-band (see illustrations).

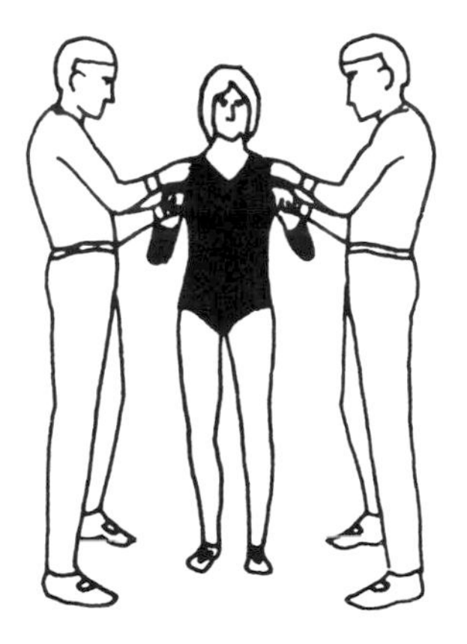

All three people bounce the bed up and down in unison ready for a take-off. You take off, aiming upwards, and at the same time displacing your hips just enough to give yourself rotational force but not so much that your head and shoulders drop. You must watch the bed during take-off, but not for so long that you have to extend your neck during the mid-flight. The body should be tucked after take-off, to speed up the rotation, and opened out for the landing. The free hands of the supporters should be placed under your seat to bring you down to a comfortable landing. If the

hand-hold support is used, the supporters should raise your hands as you land to help slow your rotation. If the waist hold is used, to slow the rotation as you descend for the landing you should raise your arms above your head. If you are rotating very swiftly, your supporters can catch you under the arms from the front, further to retard the spin.

From feet using the spotting harness

Your coach should put the belt and harness on you and check out the pulley system and your weight. He should make sure you know and understand the instructions, and agree with you the take off count. Start the jumping. You should be given some extra lift to make up for the weight of the belt.

You must take off as if there were no belt around your waist. After hip displacement, tuck to accelerate and then open out to decelerate and land.

If you are rotating a little slowly, your coach will pull on the rope to allow you more time to complete the rotation (note that the pull on the rope will also retard the rotation a little). If you are over-rotating, again your coach should pull on the rope to retard the spin and slow your descent for a comfortable landing. If the performance is just right, you will be allowed to land under control, with the ropes being left to move in time with you.

Even at this stage, your coach should be giving you instructions about unsupported performance so that you can progress towards it: the same instructions apply for performance as for hand-support or clothing-support at the waist. The belt and harness instructions are the same for the back somersault.

From feet to mat

Support should continue until you are performing more easily and need less of it. One supporter should be removed and the crash mat pushed in. When ready, you will be allowed to perform onto the mat, with a sup-

porter ready to move in from the side if needed. Gradually all support will be removed—but it should be restored if for any reason you lose your nerve. This situation may prevail for some time, until you gain real confidence from repeated success. Do not expect to learn all of the above in one or two sessions.

Progress to unsupported somersaults

This should be carried out very carefully, with proper judgement exercised at each stage. Once all support has been removed, you have to rely on your own learned ability—safety thus depends upon the quality of teaching and learning. Your coach should realise that learners can quite easily go from confidence to apprehension when performing somersaults: a fright through loss of orientation may cause a learner to request support.

You may wish to use the crash mat for the first few attempts in each practice session, even though physically the somersault is well controlled. After some time this need should disappear. The coach should ask you if you want the mat so that you can either refuse or accept without any qualms about seeming 'chicken'.

Once the supports have been discarded, a good coach will still give you psychological support through praise and encouragement, when deserved, and teaching support at all times to ensure progress. Your rate of progress will diminish gradually as your skill increases: many repetitions will be necessary for small amounts of further progress.

BACK SOMERSAULT: SKILLS AND PROGRESSIONS

Back pullover with support

For the first progression, sit on the bed leaning slightly backwards, balanced by your legs. Place your hands by the side of your head as if you were about to perform a backward roll. Pull your knees to your chest so that your body's balance is altered and you roll backwards (make sure you start the rotation like this, and *not* by pushing your shoulders backwards).

This action should roll you right up onto your shoulders; repeat it until you know the exact sequence of the movement. When you carry it out as a landing, the backwards rotation will come from the displacement of your body's centre of gravity, and will be enhanced by the bounce and accelerated by the tuck.

Next, drop from a low height with a slight gaining action, so that your seat lands on the spot where your feet were; you should be leaning slightly backwards. For this move you should be supported by a spotter to stop you opening out to land flat or taking off with rotation before you are completely ready for it.

The above landing should then be repeated with a supporter ready to help the rotation as you roll around your back and rebound just as your shoulders are reached, clearing the head. Watch you do not open out just after landing—this will effectively stop the rotation. Be careful not to

throw your head back: this leads to travel and the danger of rotating in an arc to land on your head. If the technique is followed, you will rotate easily and quickly to your feet in a low position. This will all give you practice and experience in turning backwards without needing to look backwards, trusting the techniques.

If the above is successful, increase the height of the drop so that you rebound a little higher.

Back pullover without support

To progress to unsupported back pullovers, your coach will gradually let you work more and more alone. At first, you will practise a few moves with the supporter in place; then you will be allowed to take off unassisted, with the supporter moving in after take-off. As you improve, the supporter will move in only if it is obvious from the start that you are performing the move incorrectly.

When you are working successfully, the height of the drop will gradually be increased. Transfer your arms from supporting your neck to holding onto your legs to stabilise your body for the movement. To get the idea of this, lie on your back with your legs folded so that your thighs are at right angles to your trunk and your lower legs at right angles to the upper. Your arms hold onto your thighs and your thighs push against your arms: this makes the whole trunk and upper leg a firm and stable unit. The lower leg is used to kick upwards to produce an eccentric push against the bed which gives you backward rotation.

Take off with a slightly gaining jump to land on your back, holding your legs as described above. Kick sharply into the air with your lower legs and your body will rotate round easily to feet. Normally there will be some travel, since your body does roll along the length of the back before losing contact—it is possible to perform the back pullover on the spot, but the technique is rather advanced, involving a forward kick of your legs as you land on the bed.

This move introduces unsupported backward rotation, and so is an important stage on the way to learning the back somersault, but you should certainly not yet attempt the back somersault without support.

Back somersault with support

There are a number of supports for the back somersault, each designed for a specific purpose.

Coaches should start with the learner on the trampoline and behind him a spotter with one hand on the learner's waist and the other on his neck:

the object is to give the learner the idea of initiating rotation without any danger of falling onto the bed upside down. Both learner and spotter jump together; and on the agreed signal the learner jumps into the air, displacing his hips forwards and reaching forwards and upwards so that his body rises into the air in a forward direction but rotating backwards. The spotter should push against the learner's hips to aid rotation and against his neck to avoid him dropping his shoulders. The spotter's arms should be extended as the learner reaches maximum height (see illustration). The learner is then pushed back down to stand on the bed. When the above is well ingrained, the learner should use the same take-off and, when well up in the air, tuck his body to increase rotation. The supporter should be

ready for a powerful increase in the force exerted against his arms; if necessary, he should take a step backwards to accommodate this. When the two phases of the start are mastered, move on to the next progression.

The learner stands on the bed with two spotters, one on each side. His hands are raised and the spotters grasp them as in the diagram. The other

hand of each spotter grasps the clothing at the learner's buttocks. All three jump in unison, ready for the take-off. On the agreed count the pupil jumps into the air, displacing his hips forwards at take-off so that backward rotation starts. The body should rise up, led by the knees. After about one-third of a somersault, the learner must tuck to speed up the rotation. If the take-off has been good, the tuck will enable the performer to get over the top easily. The spotters should hold the learner's seat round as far as upside-down, assisting to that point if the rotation is insufficient to ensure there is enough to get over the top. At this point they should

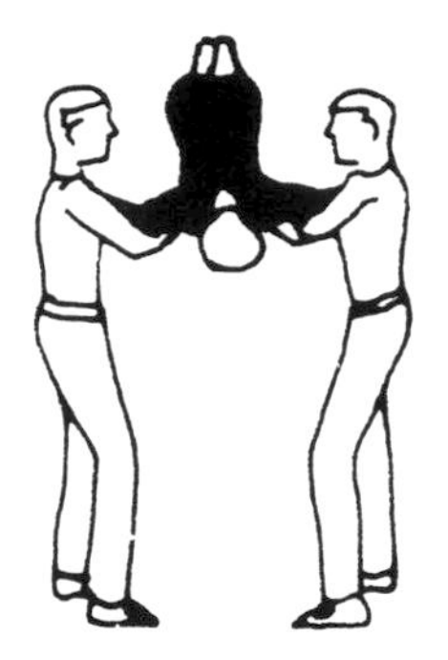

remove their hands from his seat and place them at his shoulders so that he rotates down; the supporters' hands should finish up under the pupil's shoulders as an extra support, if the rotation is short, or as a brake, if there is over-rotation.

When the learner is able to perform the move regularly, one supporter can be removed and go to the side ready to move in if necessary; the somersault is then practised with one supporter until good performance is achieved. The remaining supporter can then allow the learner to take off unsupported, stepping in to support him for the landing. Gradually, he can let the learner land with less and less actual contact. Support at the waist, by holding onto the clothing or by means of a towel or belt, can be used after the hand-holding support as a further stage before allowing the pupil to perform without support. This method is preferred by some coaches; it is also a useful addition to a supporter's repertoire.

Harness support

As an alternative to the above, the harness can be used. Check it as before (see page 52), and, by gradually removing support, progress as for the front somersault. In time, the learner can land and take off with the ropes just a little slack—but not so slack that support cannot instantly be given.

From feet to mat

The last support method used is the free take-off to land on a crash mat pushed in from the side by a spotter. This gives the learner freedom but to a large extent kills the landing, so that he does not rebound too far; also, it makes the landing comfortable if it is over- or under-rotated.

Progress to unsupported back somersaults

The problem in learning the back somersault is that if you falter you could have an accident: falling on the head or neck while rotating backwards can lead to serious injury. Because you cannot see ahead in the direction of rotation, you may suddenly become worried and hesitate at take-off. This hesitation can lead to your landing before you have completed your somersault.

Before all support is removed, both coach and pupil must be confident about success. You should not be pushed to move ahead too quickly—an inexperienced coach is more likely to do this than an experienced one. All the time the coach must reinforce progress by good teaching, so that safety is an integral part of the learning process and support can be discarded with confidence.

The weaning programme is covered in the section on front somersaults (see page 53) and in the earlier section on supporting and safety (see pages 13–16). Read both again.

FRONT SOMERSAULT WITH HALF-TWIST: SUPPORTS AND PROGRESSIONS

The coach should start the learner with a supported front somersault: this should be well lifted and not rotating too fast. Check which direction the learner twists. The support can be hand-to-hand or by harness.

If the coach is supporting by hand, he should stand on the side towards which the learner twists. He should jump with the learner, who then takes off for a tucked or piked front somersault. As the learner is opening out, the coach indicates vocally the point at which the twist is to be started. At first, the learner should merely register where the turn ought to take place.

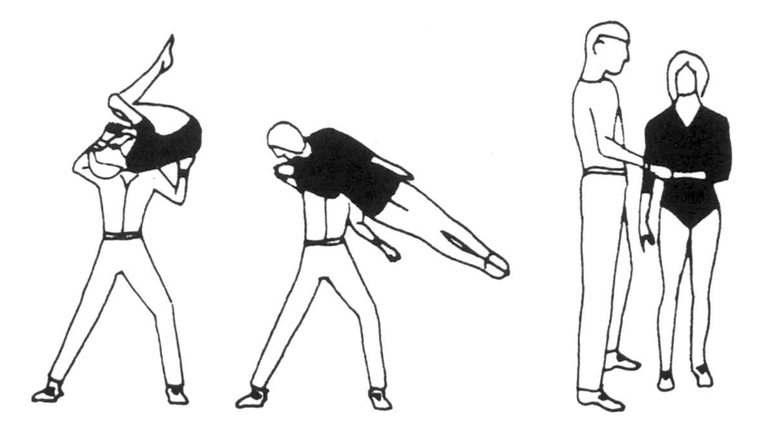

When he is ready, the somersault should be repeated, the signal given, and the learner should turn if he feels ready—if not, he should complete only a front somersault.

The turn is performed by the athlete turning his head and shoulders towards the coach as his body begins to straighten out from the tuck; the hand-hold of the coach gives some stability for the learner to turn against. After practice, he should be able easily to complete the half-twist and land under control. Visual contact with the bed is not possible with the late twist: some beginners find this a problem.

The same move can be carried out in the twisting harness. The learner again needs a good front somersault—not too fast—and the direction of the twist must be the same as for all other moves incorporating twists. The coach should check the point of twist and the readiness of the learner to attempt the whole movement. Support is as before.

The barani

The barani is a special name for a front somersault with a half-twist in which the learner keeps visual contact with the bed throughout the move. Some coaches suggest learners should first perform Arab springs on the bed to get a good idea of the move, but this in most cases leads to a pulled-down start and, often, a mistaken impression of the direction of twist. If you can do the front somersault with half-twist, you will already know the correct direction of twist.

With either hand or harness support, the coach should encourage you to start the twist a little earlier and to try to watch the bed as the somersault progresses. You should lift upwards into the movement rather than let it be pulled down. A fast learner will move ahead steadily, and will soon be able to see the bed throughout; the slower learner will perhaps move ahead

and then regress a little. The coach must keep repeating the move, encouraging you to twist a little earlier, still using support. A small amount of kip or lift of the harness will help to get the extra height and power the learner often loses through a lack of skill or confidence.

Once you have mastered the visual problem you will usually have mastered the barani. Both types of twist will then be available to you. Remember that the barani in which the twist is initiated at take-off will lead into all forward early-twisting single and double somersaults, and that the late-twisting front somersault with half-twist is the same type of twist as the barani out and rudi out fliffus. It is thus well worth practising both skills.

As before, the gradual removal of support from hand or harness to crash mat and then to free take-off and landing must be pursued with care. The success of future endeavours will depend upon the quality of learning and performance of both the skills and the moves which stem from them.

Competitive trampolining

LEVELS OF COMPETITIVE TRAMPOLINING

In Britain, trampolining is mainly a recreational activity, but competition is also important. The BTF runs a national squad and other zonal squads from which are selected teams for international matches, the ultimate objective being the European and World Championships. These are held bi-annually: the European Championships take place on the odd dates and the World Championships on the even dates. Additionally, annual international programmes are arranged in Europe, on the American continent and for the Pacific countries (Australia, New Zealand and Japan). In Europe, international competitions are arranged in Britain, Czechoslovakia, France, Holland, Poland, Russia, Switzerland and West Germany. This provides a balanced international programme throughout the year.

The International Trampoline Federation is the governing body for the sport throughout the world. Twenty-six nations are members, and this figure is increasing annually. The member nations are (early 1983) Australia, Austria, Belgium, Canada, Czechoslovakia, Denmark, Finland, France, Great Britain, Hong Kong, Ireland, Japan, Luxembourg, the Netherlands, New Zealand, Poland, Portugal, Scotland, South Africa, Spain, Sweden, Switzerland, USA, USSR, Venezuela and West Germany.

In the UK competitors are catered for at all levels. There is an annual England/Wales/Scotland/Northern Ireland international match. National Championships are held in the categories Open, Under-18, Under-15, Under-13 and Under-11. Divisional open competitions and divisional closed competitions are held in the same categories in eight divisions. The national open championships in Wales, Scotland and Northern Ireland are open to all, as is the British Trampoline Federation Open. There is also a Schools' National Championship, run in the form of an elimination competition and open to all schools. Synchronised trampoline competitions are at present run only at international and national open level. There are many schools' competitions run by county associations, and in the London area there is a trampoline league.

There is still room for more development of competitive trampolining at the very lowest level, to cater for beginners who may never attain some of the high standards of performance displayed even at club competitions. Some trampoline clubs run invitation competitions which are very well attended.

TRAINING AND FITNESS

Those who intend to compete should attend at least three training sessions per week. Practice at trampolining uses up quite a lot of time, and any group wishing to compete should have at least two trampolines: this ensures, too, that synchronised trampolining can be performed if desired. Trampolining requires a high level of performance, and many, many repetitions of each movement are needed to achieve competence.

The training programme should be designed with two objectives: skills and fitness. The organised coach will have an outline programme to develop learners from beginners to competent performers. Training is not just practice but practice to a pattern, with advice on performance, on learning new skills, and on development of necessary strength and endurance for performance when that little extra must be drawn out to win.

Practice must be observed and analysed, changed where necessary and repeated where necessary. The introduction to new moves must be planned and brought about at the right stage of development. All coaches should make charts of performance levels and of failures, with analyses of the reasons for failure and plans for correction. A planned programme does not guarantee being a regular winner—that may depend upon the quality of the opposition—but it will help to better your performance.

Fitness should come with training. Fitness in any activity means the preparation of the body's physiological systems to meet the practical physical demands of the sport without failure through lack of breath, tiredness of the major muscular systems of the body, or fatigue. Many textbooks deal with fitness, and the wise coach should at least look through some to see if there is anything useful in them. Other available books deal with the principles of learning skills. The information should prove of use to coaches who do not have a physical-education background or a basic knowledge of that subject.

To a certain extent, respiratory fitness will be improved by the act of jumping on the trampoline during practice. However, the serious competitor should take some steps towards working specifically for the endurance which comes with respiratory fitness. Jumping on the trampoline is strenuous if the jumps are high with good body tension and many changes of body shape. Instead of running for two minutes, the performers should jump for two minutes, performing simple moves. Double bouncing increases the use of the equipment, and capable performers can handle this safely. Two sessions of two or three minutes each will increase the capacity of the heart and lungs. This is nowadays called 'aerobic exercise'.

Although some skills require concentration in addition to physical effort, it is important that the simpler skills are practised frequently. Not only does this serve as endurance training, it also fixes good form in the performer's system.

STRENGTH-BUILDING

An increase in strength is normally an advantage to anyone involved in sport. Not only does it help the trampolinist jump better and hold body positions in flight, it helps prevent injury by increasing both support to the joints and muscle mobility.

As with fitness, some strength improvement will come from the normal programme on the trampoline. Considerable strength is needed for superior performance, and often poor form can be in part attributed to a lack of it.

The use of weights or exercise machines is the best way to increase strength. Programmes can be designed purely to increase strength or to increase strength with endurance. These are basically for the serious trampolinist, but will benefit anyone who uses them. Care must be taken with very young performers (aged 9 to 12) not to damage the developing joints through too intense work with heavy resistance. The young will, however, benefit from specific exercises which use their own body weights rather than artificial weights.

There are three main principles involved in gaining strength: (1) progressive overload, (2) specific adaptation to changing demands, and (3) gradual strength-loss when training ceases. A general strength-training programme with work for each of the main muscle groups is a good start for any performer, supplemented by specific training as the performer gets more skilled and performance demands become more particular. The main needs must be analysed and a programme of work developed accordingly. In trampolining, the leg, lower-back and abdominals are the main working muscles, with the arm and shoulder muscles under less loading. However, the body must be worked in a balanced way to avoid any possible injury resulting from over-developing a single group of muscles.

Strength increases through the stimulation of more and more muscle fibres through progressive overload. Many coaches and learners progress too quickly in a strength-training programme and as a result *overwork* the muscular groups. Overwork results in too high a level of fatigue, poor strength gain and possible injury through strain. Overwork can result from too many workouts, too much overloading, and too little rest between work on the different muscle groups during the workouts.

Strength-gain is *between* workouts. There must be time between them to allow for this—no more than three sessions per week should be undertaken in the close season and two during the season.

For those aged under 10 (and up to 12, depending on the learner's physical development), in order to avoid injury to the developing joints it is better to use body-weight exercises. These provide a suitable level of work without the danger of strain. From 13 to 15 some weights can be used: they should be light and the emphasis should be on plenty of repetitions for endurance with only a little work on strength. From 15 upwards, heavier weights can be used to get real strength-gains. With the young, it is better to err on the lighter side than the heavier.

To plan a programme, the coach needs to analyse the main muscle groups used in the sport and to work on those specifically. Before any specific work is done, the main muscular groups should be strengthened using a general strength-gaining programme.

Work should be on the large groups first, remembering that the abdominals and the lower-back muscles are usually used as stabilisers for many other muscle actions and so should be worked on last in the programme. Small specific muscle groups will cramp more easily than large ones, and should be worked on first.

In order to keep a balanced development of strength, work is needed on both sides of the main joints; e.g., thighs and hamstrings, stomach and spine muscles. This will help avoid injury through an imbalance of strengths in the large muscle groups.

TRAINING PRINCIPLES

In order to be systematic, a programme must be designed according to certain principles which can be followed easily by the learner (without having to resort to complicated calculations) and which can easily be entered upon his record card.

The technique is to work the muscle smoothly and without jerking throughout its whole range, starting from fully stretched. It is not good practice to use a short range of movement when a muscle has a large range. Work until no further contractions can be achieved. Keep to the prescribed order of exercise.

If the coach is using the maximum-repetitions concept to regulate training, he should find the weight the athlete can just lift, with good form, about six times (if working for strength) or ten times (if working for endurance). Aim for about a fifty per cent increase in repetitions as a measure of progress; e.g., nine or ten repetitions where before there were only six. When the maximum can just be reached, it is time to increase the weight.

There is no reason why the number of repetitions indicated above cannot be exceeded during training: the important thing is to design the programme so that generally the number set cannot easily be exceeded without work over a period of time. This means that each athlete's personal programme will probably contain a different number of repetitions. The number should be such that the pupil is able to lift the weight no more than one or two repetitions more than or less than the maximum until training has taken place and it is obvious that the weight needs to be increased.

The programme

The programme should take account of the following:

- ☐ what exercises are to be performed
- ☐ the order in which the muscle groups are to be exercised
- ☐ the maximum number of repetitions to be used (strength or endurance)
- ☐ the number of sets to be used
- ☐ the time interval between exercises and sets of exercises
- ☐ the number of training sessions per week (in season and out of season); note that strength will decrease as less work is done

Safety in weight training

Most gymnasia or multi-gym rooms have safety rules. These are usually on the wall. If there are none, get some put up. If this is not possible, they should be on the training card given to each athlete. A sample set of rules follows: these are basic and could be added to (see also page 12).

- ☐ no fooling around
- ☐ wear trainers, socks and vest or shirt
- ☐ check and tighten the collars at the ends of the bars
- ☐ use others who are training to support weights if necessary (they can also encourage you)
- ☐ breathe in before starting to lift and breathe out during the lift
- ☐ wear a support for heavy squats or dead lifts

It is important that you should know how to use the weights, and all coaches should run a short induction course. This course should include:

- ☐ an explanation of the principles of weight training
- ☐ taking the weight measurements and strength levels of each learner
- ☐ covering the safety rules
- ☐ covering the exercises to be performed and demonstrating them
- ☐ explanation of the purpose of the exercises
- ☐ explanation of the use of the record cards, and their filling-in
- ☐ getting the athletes to go over the exercises, using and teaching good form

General programme for major muscle groups

Listed in the table overleaf are the major muscle groups and exercises for them using either free weights or the multi-gym (exercise machine). For trampolining, the main groups to exercise are the legs, the abdominals and lower-back muscles, and the arms and shoulders. Some work should be done on the muscles at the sides of the abdomen, which are used in twisting. A general programme for all-round strength should be used before specific work is carried out on the 'trampoline muscles'. Remember that before all workouts there should be a warm-up (see pages 68 – 69) to avoid tears or injury to muscles and joints. Make sure that the safety rules are observed at all times. Remember that progress is made through *effort* and *correctly performed exercises*.

From the exercises listed in the table, specific ones may be selected to correct weaknesses, to improve power for jumping, or to increase strength in the mid-section for holding straight positions in flight, tucking more quickly or using the arms effectively at take-off or during good phased twisting. One could design a general workout to develop the areas mentioned, drawing attention to trampoline-muscle needs and helping the athletes learn a little more about the other aspects of the sport, which they may in time be able to pass on to pupils of their own.

anatomical name	*common name*	*free weights*	*multi-gym*
gluteals	buttocks	stiff-leg deadlift	back hyper-extension
quadriceps	thighs (front)	squat	leg press
hamstrings	thighs (back)	leg curls	leg curls
gastrocnemius	calves	calf raise	toe presses
pectorals	chest muscles	bench press	bench press, dips
latissimus dorsi	large muscles on side of chest	bent-over rowing, bent-arm pullover	pulldowns, chins
deltoids	shoulders	upright rowing	upright rowing
biceps	upper arm (front)	curls	curls, chins
triceps	upper arm (back)	arm extensions	arm extensions on pulldown bar, dips
abdominals	stomach muscles	sit-ups (bench variable slope)	sit-ups (bench variable slope)
spinal muscles	long back muscles	side-bends (dumb-bells)	side-bends (bench press station)

WARM-UP

Warming-up is for safety reasons provided for in the rules of trampoline competitions (see page 78). Two hours must be allowed for a general warm-up before the competition, and each competitor must have a thirty-second warm-up before each routine. It is felt that each competitor should be allowed to go over beforehand the compulsory and the voluntary routine to avoid injury from muscle action and also to avoid, as far as possible, the chance of injury through failure during a difficult routine.

However, there is no real scientific evidence that warming-up does contribute to physical performance. A considerable amount of research has been carried out in recent years, but the evidence is unfortunately inconclusive. Some researchers have felt that warming-up is beneficial, others that it makes little or no difference. However, this is not the place to cover all the aspects of warm-up research.

Since warming-up is included in the rules, it is wise to take advantage of the allowance. It gives the opportunity for last-minute practice at high or low level, as desired by the competitor. It gives you the chance to raise the temperature of your body and, theoretically, to make muscle contraction and relaxation faster and stronger because of lower viscosity within the muscle. It can help avoid muscle tears due to irregular rates of contraction and relaxation between opposing muscle groups, or to lack of synchronisation between the messages to the muscle groups in use for specific moves.

What is important is that most coaches and performers *believe* warming-up to be beneficial, and are unhappy to compete without due allowance for it. It thus has a psychological effect for the better on performers, and should be included. There is no evidence at all that warming-up has a *bad* effect!

Briefly, it is believed that your warm-up needs to be shortly before your performance, and sufficient to raise the temperature of your body a little (hence the name) but not to fatigue you. It is *not* a substitute for practice or the learning of routines. Competitors should not be trying to learn at the last moment moves which they have not perfected during training. Performers who use the warm-up period for this purpose tend not to be winners.

PSYCHOLOGICAL PREPARATION

For most tests it is important to be psychologically prepared. Learning new moves and taking part in competitions are tests—tests of the performer's ability to concentrate and to repeat or add together previously practised sections of a routine or skill while under pressure. What is needed to pass these tests? If the physical preparation is equal to the task, what will determine success or failure? Usually, it is psychological preparedness.

The role of the team manager or coach is to see to all preparations for the competitor, so that the competitor has nothing to worry about during the competition. Preparation includes such things as travel, food, clothing, accommodation and the actual participation. It starts long beforehand. The routine has to be decided upon and practised. The faults have to be found and eradicated, and together both performer and coach have to feel that the preparation has been done well and a reasonable level of success is to be expected; that is, the athlete should have certain expectations that are no higher than his or her sensibly estimated standard of performance. Conversely, athletes should not be expected to perform below their proper standards.

At all levels of performance, trampolinists are working at or near their top ability. Unlike many other sports, there are no rest periods during the actual performance. Even in the compulsory routine—normally technically easier than the voluntary routine—there is still a striving for perfect form: very good height, good phasing, and no travel.

The wise coach will instil calm confidence in the athlete rather than a 'psyched-up' state. To do this the coach will have to display calm confidence as well—the performer has enough to contend with without having to deal with a nervous coach! Anger from a coach will not help if things are not going well, and neither will recriminations afterwards. The athlete should not be expected to perform much better (or worse) than in the training sessions.

It is true that many coaches—especially parents—have expectations beyond the athletes' abilities, while at the same time possibly lacking confidence in the athlete. They then put pressure on the performer and try to 'rig' the competition in small ways—making a fuss about the equipment, the warm-up arrangements, the spotters or advantages apparently gained by other competitors. These attitudes adversely affect the athletes at a time when they need to be concentrating on performance.

If a performer has failed, he or she should have no need to fear the coach's reactions. The reasons for failure should be analysed, and subsequent training sessions should be designed to avoid a similar failure next time. Both coach and athlete should also realise that failure sometimes occurs out of the blue. Try to accept these blows of fate philosophically.

THE COMPETITION

To those who take the sport seriously, the competition is the culmination of all the months of training and preparation. All preparation must be finished, and the athlete should be confident about his or her chances of success—getting first place, beating a near rival, or just going for a result somewhere along the line between the least good and the best. Whatever the goal, it should be a realistic one.

The last training session should be primarily to reassure the performers that they are ready and have learned their routines well. There should be no rushing to get a new move ready during the last few days of training.

All clothing, sandwiches, drinks, etc., should be ready the night before, especially if a very early start is needed; the route should be worked out in advance. Make sure the car is full of petrol, oil and water, and that the battery is charged-up. If going by minibus or coach, confirm the pick-up arrangements. Check about accommodation.

Set off for the venue in good time. Make sure that the warm-up period for your particular event is not missed. Check in case there are any alterations to the previously stated programme. Complete the competition card (see rule 7). If the coach discovers any problems, he or she should not communicate any worry or annoyance to the performer.

Coaches should make sure that they have clearly in their minds the times of their athletes' performances, and that the athletes are ready in good time for their sections. They should not disappear, leaving the athletes confused as to what is going on. It is a good idea if they give out some written instructions to their protégés about the day's events, *confirmed after arrival at the competition venue*, so that each one has the latest information available and there is no need for them to go rushing around panic-stricken should their coach happen not to be present for a little while.

As the athlete gets onto the trampoline, the coach should maintain a calm and confident look, so that no uncertainty of any kind is transmitted. When the routine is finished, the coach should stay calm, whether it was a success or failure—especially if it was a failure. It is probably best to talk generally about the day's events and leave the inquest until later. The performer will have had enough for one day and should be allowed to have some fun.

At the next training session the failure or success can be discussed. Success is easier to handle than failure: keep to the successful routine and lay plans for further progress. If the performer has failed, the coach should analyse the reasons and work to correct them, so that the same failure is avoided in the next competition.

4
Judging

THE SCORING SYSTEM

Trampoline competitions consist of one compulsory and two voluntary routines. The trampoline scoring system is marked in tenths of a point for form (how you do it), difficulty (what it consists of), and, in synchronised competitions, synchronisation (staying together).

☐ In individual competitions, the highest and lowest scores given by the five form judges are deleted, and the remaining three scores are added together.
☐ In synchronised competitions, the highest and lowest scores of the three judges for each competitor are deleted, and the middle scores for each competitor added together.
☐ Each competitor's performance scores in each round are added together to get individual totals. The same system is used for each pair in synchronised competitions.
☐ The difficulty scores (tariffs) for the voluntary routine(s) are added to the performance scores. Some deductions may have to be made. (See below.)
☐ Each extra straight jump in a voluntary routine will be penalised by the deduction of 1 point.
☐ Lack of synchronisation will be marked by deductions of
  ☐ 0.1-0.3 points for landing differences up to 50 cm;
  ☐ 0.4-0.5 points for landing differences over 50 cm.

Difficulty or tariff

The tariff, or degree of difficulty, in a trampoline routine is assessed in tenths of a point as follows.

- ☐ If there is no rotation no tariff score is given.
- ☐ For somersaults 0.1 of a point is given for each quarter of a somersault (i.e., 90 degrees' rotation). Thus a full somersault (360 degrees) gets 0.4 points.
- ☐ For twists, 0.1 of a point is given for each half-twist (180 degrees). Thus 0.2 is given for a full twist (360 degrees).
- ☐ For twisting somersaults, the tariff for the somersault is added to the tariff for the twists.
- ☐ For piked and straight somersaults of 360 degrees or more without twist, an extra tenth of a point is added.
- ☐ Piked and straight somersaults of 720 degrees (two full turns) or more with twists add an extra tenth of a point (the legs must be kept straight at all times).

For each competitor (or, in the synchronised competition, pair of competitors), the scores from the two/three rounds are added, after all deductions have been made, to get the final score.

HOW THE ROUTINES ARE ASSESSED FOR FORM

The required positions in a routine are set out in the rules (see below). However, only with the publication of the International Trampoline Federation *Handbook* (1982) have any written guidelines been published. That said, the published guidelines still need refinement, since they can cause confusion. Trampolining is a young sport and will have to develop further before everyone has been able to make up their minds about what is good form and what is merely fashion. Nevertheless, improvements are being made all the time to enable judges to keep up with the talents of those coaches and performers who are inventive and forward-looking.

Only 0.5 of the point available for each move can be deducted. This means that, if a competitor completes ten moves, a score of 5 is guaranteed. Effectively, routines are marked between 5 and 10 points.

The required positions

Certain positions are specified in the rules and these must be executed according to the specifications or deductions will be made. In a compulsory routine, the requirements *must* be met otherwise the routine will be terminated at the point when they are not. This applies to the positions of *tuck pike* and *straight*. In voluntary routines, a repeat move may be called, and tariff is lost for that move.

With regard to the legs, arms, knees, feet and toes, lack of attention in these areas may mean, throughout the routine, loss of form-marks. The star performer, however, is able to inject a 'something' in performance which is not written down anywhere but which can be recognised immediately. This may be called style, flair or presentation: it is a combination of many things and some performers never achieve it.

The requirements are:

- ☐ In tucked, piked and straight positions the feet, legs and knees *must* be kept together, and the feet and toes pointed.
- ☐ In the tucked and piked positions the upper body *must* be kept at an angle of not more than 90 degrees to the thighs (except in the twisting phase of the somersault).
- ☐ In the tucked position the hands *must* grasp the shins below the knees (except in the twisting phase).
- ☐ In the pucked position the thighs *must* be kept at an angle of between 90 and 120 degrces to the upper body.
- ☐ The pucked position can be used only in the twisting phase of double (and more) somersaults.
- ☐ Arm position and movement is free but should be straight whenever possible.
- ☐ The same move in both the tucked and pucked positions is considered a repeat, for which there is loss of tariff.

MAKING THE BEST OF YOUR PRESENTATION

After the preparation that goes into a competitive routine, it is best to try to ensure that it is not all wasted by poor presentation on the day. As a judge and spectator at many national and international competitions over the last couple of decades, I have noticed that many talented performers give away marks too easily.

Firstly, dress smartly in a clean, well fitting outfit. Many boys have badly fitting white trousers and leotards; many girls have leotards which climb higher and higher up their thighs and need to be pulled down. Often trampoline shoes are not clean.

Get onto the trampoline and stand ready for the signal to start. If you have to adjust the pads, do so quickly and go back to the centre of the bed.

Learn to perform your build-up jumps under control and with good stretch: the judges are already watching and forming an impression. If you feel out of control, stop and start again—provided that you have not yet made a move. This is better than making attempts to regain control over a long period of jumping, which may tire you and cause loss of concentration.

Try not to travel or lose height. Remember that, if you do, it may be better to put in an easy jump which helps you regain control than to struggle along with a routine which seems to be getting more difficult as you progress through it and ends up as a mad struggle for balance. Often a single tuck jump will give you enough time to recover and to continue under control.

At the end of the routine, stand still for three seconds (count them silently using some such system as 'one thousand and one, two thousand and two, three thousand and three'). Many competitors lose 0.1 or more for failing to satisfy this simple demand: this deduction, being trebled, can make a lot of difference to your final score. If you are the coach, remember not to speak to the performer until the three seconds are up: it can cost him or her 0.3 of a point every time you speak.

5

The rules for the competitor

There are a number of rules which every competitor and coach should know, so that there is an awareness of what is allowed and what is not: this can clear up many misunderstandings about what happens at competitions and also enables better preparation to take place. Some of the rules about scoring and so on have already been mentioned. The ones set out below are for the competitor to know and in the main act by when out on the trampoline. Knowledge of these may also enable the coach to be able to put in a reasonable protest if any rules have been broken and the placings of the competitors thereby affected. The entirety of the rule is not given unless necessary, only that part of it relating directly to the competitor.

Synchronised competitions

3.4 The compulsory routine of the individual competition is also the compulsory routine in the synchronised competition.

3.5 The competitors have to do the same movement at the same time in the same rhythm and must start facing in the same direction. Synchronised partners need not twist in the same direction.

Routines

5.2 Second attempts at routines are not allowed.

5.3 If a competitor is obviously disturbed in a routine (faulty equipment or external influence), the jury is called together by the superior judge and a second attempt may be allowed by a majority vote.

This situation will normally be covered automatically by the superior judge (referee), but a coach could protest on this one.

Dress for individual and synchronised competitors as well as official spotters

6.1 *Men.* For each country a uniform gym shirt without sleeves, long white gym trousers and white gym shoes or white foot covering must be worn.

(A gym shirt is a leotard or tee-shirt. Normally, shorts may be worn in competitions. Gym shoes are trampoline shoes or non-slip foot coverings.)

6.2 *Ladies.* For each country a uniform leotard and white gym shoes or white foot covering of no more than ankle length must be worn.

(This means that knee socks should not be worn. The referee will soon let you know if you are out of order.)

6.4 No jewellery or watches shall be permitted to be worn during the competition.
6.5 Any violation of these rules (**6.1/2/4**) will result in disqualification. The superior judge makes the decision.

Competition cards

7.1 The voluntary routine and the difficulty rating must be written on the competition card.
7.2 The competition card must be given to the recorder at least two hours before the competition starts.
7.3 Changes are permitted during the voluntary routine.

(Some competitions do not have competition cards issued before the day of the competition. Make sure that you or your coach gets the card and hands it in to the officials in good time.)

Safety

10.3 The competitor may request from the superior judge his own spotters.
10.4 The competitors must execute their routines without any external help.
10.5 Talking to the competitors by their own spotters or coach during the routine is not permitted. Each time this rule is disregarded, it will result in the deduction of 0.3 points by the assistant superior judge and performance judges no. 1-6 at the instruction of the superior judge.

(It is important to realise that each competitor may have personal spotters for routines. It *must* be remembered by the spotters and coach that talking is not permitted. 0.3 is a large deduction and can make the difference between a win and a defeat.)

Protests

13.1 A protest can only be handed in by an official representative of a federation, a team manager, competitor or coach.
13.2 A written protest with the protest fee must be handed to the superior judge before the end of the round.
13.3 Performance scores in individual and synchronised competitions as well as non-synchronised deductions can only be protested if there is a numerical error.

(Note on **13.3**: if you do not like the score you cannot protest, but if it has been added up wrongly you should protest.)

Warming-up

14.1 Before the start of the competition, training on the competition apparatus of at least two hours must be given.
14.2 All competitors will be allowed one practice of 30 seconds before each round in which he participates.

(Unless this has been altered in the pre-competition information, make sure that it takes place.)

Start of routine

15.1 Each competitor will start on the signal given by the superior judge.
15.2 A competitor may take as many preliminary jumps as he desires before commencing the first skill.
15.3 If there is a faulty start prior to the first skill caused by slipping, falling, legs buckling, etc., the athlete shall be allowed to leave the trampoline and to start again with no penalty, subject to the approval of the superior judge.

(Too many preliminary jumps may not help you get the best start. Make a habit of going into the take-off after no more than five or six jumps.)

Repetition of the same skills

17.1 During the voluntary routine the same skill must not be repeated.
17.2 If the competitor disregards this rule, the degree of difficulty of the repeated skill will not be counted.
17.3 Multiple somersaults (of more than 360 degrees) with the same number of twists and somersaults are considered to have the same degree of difficulty. When the twist is located in a different phase of the skill, this is not considered to be a repetition.
17.4 Tucked, piked or straight positions are considered to be different skills and not repetitions.

Interruptions of the routine

18.1 A routine is considered to be interrupted if the competitor
18.1.1 Does not perform the compulsory routine in the written sequence or as prescribed.
18.1.2 Obviously does not land simultaneously on both feet on the trampoline bed.
18.1.3 Does not use the elasticity of the bed after landing for the immediate continuation of the next movement, thus causing a break.
18.1.4 During the routine touches anything other than the bed with any part of the body. This decision must be made by the jury.
18.1.5 Is touched physically by any spotter. This decision is made by the superior judge.
18.1.6 During the routine leaves the trampoline due to insecurity.
18.1.7 Performs a routine different skill from that of his partner in the synchronised routine.
18.2 A competitor will be judged only on the number of skills completed on the trampoline bed.

Termination of the routine

19.1 The routine must end with both feet on the trampoline bed.
19.2 The competitor is allowed to do one more jump in a stretched position.
19.3 If the competitor does not land upright on both feet on the bed, a deduction will be made by the performance judges.

19.4 For additional skills a deduction of a total of 1.0 will be made by the assistant superior judge and the performance judges on the instructions of the superior judge.

19.5 The competitor must stand upright after his last landing on the bed for at least three seconds, otherwise he will receive a deduction from the assistant superior judge and performance judges no. 1-6 for insecurity. (See rules 23.3.2)

Deductions for faulty performance

23.3 Deductions for faulty performance.

23.3.1 For each skill for lack of individual constant height poor execution and control, *0.1-0.5*.

23.3.2 For lack of control on or after the last bounce.

23.3.2.1 landing on one foot only, *0.3*

23.3.2.2 additional steps after landing on both feet on the bed and not standing still for 3 secs., *0.1-0.3*

23.3.2.3 touching the bed with one hand, *0.4*

23.3.2.4 touching the bed with both hands, *0.5*

23.3.2.5 landing on the knees or hands and knees, *0.6*

23.3.2.6 landing on the seat, *0.7*

23.3.2.7 landing on the stomach or back, *0.8*

23.3.2.8 touching or landing on the suspension system, pads or frame, *0.9*

23.3.2.9 for falling off the trampoline at any time after the first skill of the routine, *1.0*

(The coach and pupil who know the values of the above deductions may be able to save some points if they are aware of the situation. For instance, it may be easy to land on the seat instead of on the back—it saves a tenth of a point in the table; however, remember the score is trebled, meaning that the deduction will be 0.3—a considerable loss.)

6

The mini-tramp and double mini-tramp

As an aid to diving

Like the trampoline, the mini-tramp (a compact piece of equipment having a frame size of about 110cm (3ft 8in) square) can be used as an aid to diving—and at far less expense. The same moves can be practised, with a little adaptation of the run for forward moves, and the standing take-off for backward moves. The advantage is that, once it is set up (with two or three crash mats), many learners can practise the moves in quick succession in the gym without having to hire or travel to a pool. It is not possible to perform head-first landings, any more than it is on the trampoline, but the athlete can turn over onto his or her back (going forwards) or front (going backwards). What is useful is the take-off practice, the phasing of the moves in the air, and the effects of constant repetition on the athlete's fitness.

If the bed of the mini-tramp is levelled and a run-up area at the same height is prepared (e.g., two benches with a mat covering), an even better simulation of the diving situation is available.

As an aid to gymnastics

Although the mini-tramp is not specifically designed for gymnastics, it can be a cheap aid for the practising of somersaults, with or without twists. It may be more useful than the trampoline, since it is more difficult to attain too much height. It does give height and power, though, and may be used with the belt—the belt can be used more easily for backward than for forward work, since there is no run-up for backward skills.

As in diving, it is most useful as a training aid to give the athlete practice which is relatively easy, owing to the readily available power. It will *not*, however, solve all problems.

As an activity for schools

The use of the mini-tramp has been banned by some local authorities, but for no good reason. It is easy and, if reasonable precautions are taken, it is safe. It is important that there are crash mats for landing and that progressions are used (see below). The activity can be one section of a PE class, and can occupy quite a number of pupils quickly. It does get them used to height and flight, and can be used also for vaulting by those pupils who are not able easily to get height from the springboard, reuther board or floor. It can be used also to practise moves like the jump to handstand by intermediate-level performers who may not need to run up to the box every time.

Supporting on the mini-tramp is easy for front and back somersaults, so that pupils can safely be taught to provide it. This can allow many youngsters who might never have been able to attempt a somersault to experience the thrill of this move.

Only the most experienced performers should be allowed to attempt double somersaults, either forwards or backwards. By 'experienced' I mean those who can already perform these moves on the trampoline. Remember that height is easily obtainable on the mini-tramp in comparison with work on the floor, but not in comparison with work on the trampoline.

The double mini-tramp

The double mini-tramp is a development of the mini-tramp; its use has become a sport in the USA, some European countries, Australia, and South Africa. It is a piece of equipment with more possibilities than the mini-tramp, and a number of people can use it in a short space of time.

Basically it is a long resilient bed about 400mm (16in) from the ground with an open-ended frame at each end. It is possible to perform moves on the bed after a run-up and then a move off the bed onto a crash mat or other resilient surface. It is fun and physically demanding, and even beginners can have a safe and enjoyable time using the power and flight available from it.

Like the mini-tramp, it is approached with a short run-up and a hurdle-step take-off. At first it is used just for jumping on, performing a second jump, and then jumping off, but those used to the mini-tramp can jump on and perform a move on the second jump. The most advanced performers can perform double somersaults on the bed after the first landing and then double-somersault off.

Competitions are similar to trampoline competitions—a compulsory exercise is performed followed by a voluntary routine; these are marked for form, height and control. The double mini-tramp can be used as expertly by tumblers as by trampolinists; and, obviously, some people opt for double mini-tramp work only.

In a school, the equipment can be used as a mini-tramp but offering more versatility. Safety must be observed, and once again support can be given by trained pupils as well as by the teacher. Somersaults on the apparatus must only be attempted by those who are already proficient at them on the trampoline.

Safety and supporting

The safety of the learner is the most important element of sports such as trampolining and gymnastics. This applies to all offshoots of these sports.

Crash mats are essential. It is not enough to have ordinary gym mats on the floor, unless simple jumps only are being performed—and it is far better to have the thicker mats even for simple jumps. Always use spotters—either, for simple work, trained pupils or, for advanced work, the teacher or coach. It may be necessary to have two spotters—the teacher and a competent pupil can do this. It may be necessary to have two thicknesses of crash mat for first attempts at new moves, with a further mat at the far end in case of over-rotation and a long flight.

When learners first run up, or even walk up, to take their first jumps on both mini-tramp and double mini-tramp, they should have been shown how to hold their bodies. It is important not to let the hips get ahead of the feet at take-off; otherwise the hips may be pushed further forward, causing the learner to land with an arched back and possibly fall backwards onto the frame. The back must be held straight and the legs well stretched: this ensures that the push from the bed goes in a straight line up the legs and spine, avoiding a strong push in the wrong direction.

Start with simple jumps, aiming for height and not distance. Have spotters ready to stop learners from over-rotating or falling over when the feet stop after long-distance low jumps. Somersaults must be supported. Front somersaults can be supported by a belt around the waist and two supporters, or by two supporters using hand-hold or waist support. For first attempts the pupil can jump up and down on the mini-tramp and double mini-tramp. The running start should be attempted after some competence has been gained using the stationary start.

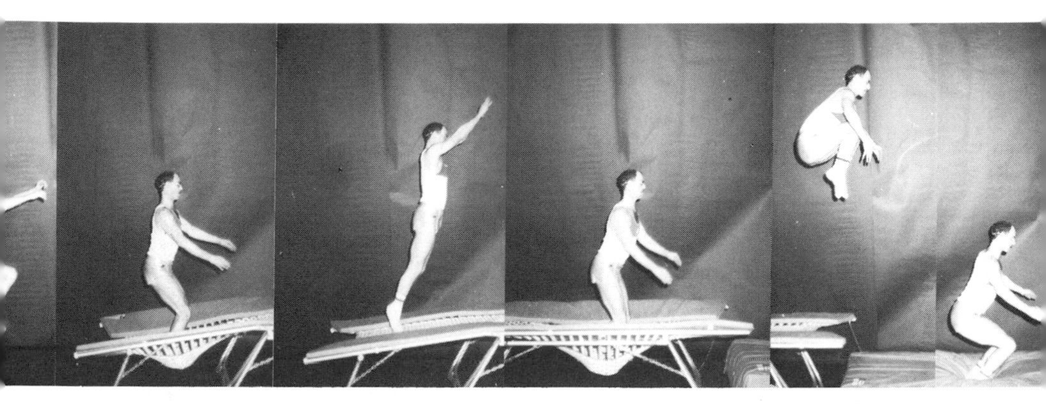

For back somersaults, two supporters using the belt or waist grip will ensure good support. At first, the supporters may find it easier to put one foot on the front edge of the apparatus to stop the learner leaning out too far.

At all times it is wise to have spotters standing by for landings. This can

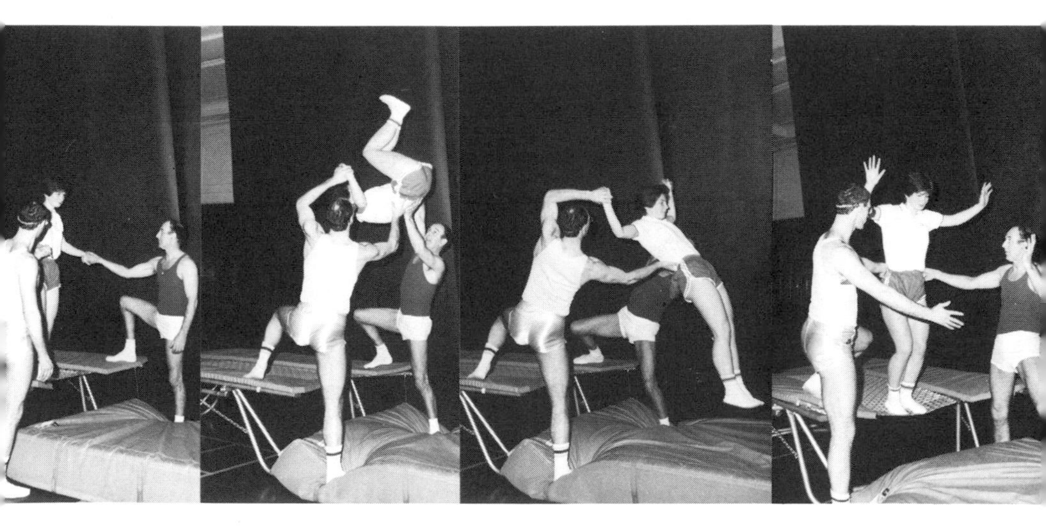

be arranged by having the preceding performers staying at the apparatus or by having two stay for one round. Make sure that the duties are clearly set out and practised before serious work begins.

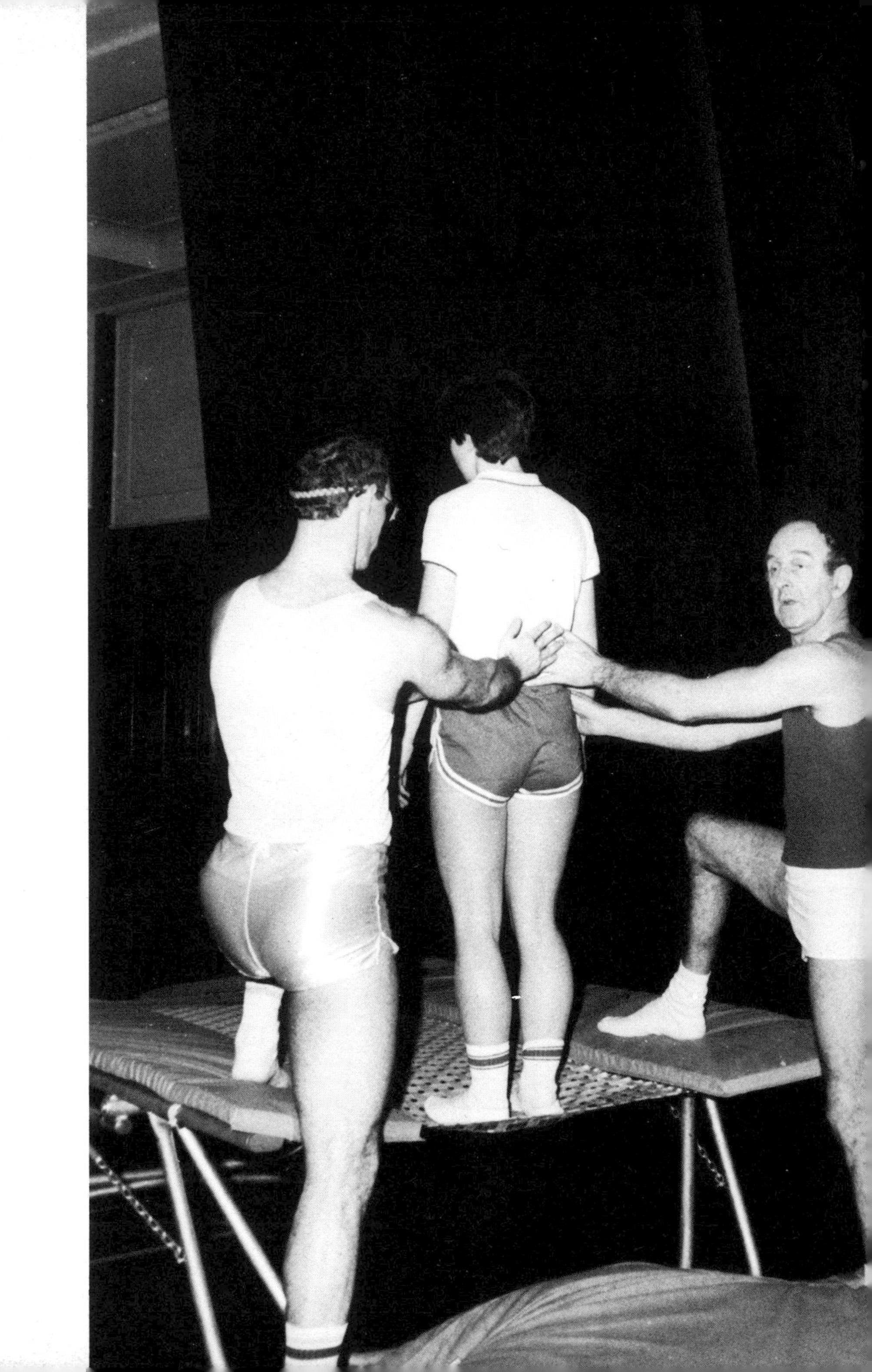

Appendix 1

Running a competition

BEFORE THE COMPETITION

Many people think a competition just happens: what they fail to realise is that considerable effort goes into setting up even a bad one. A little thought beforehand will help ensure that all this work is not wasted. Here are the requirements, so that you can check them off as they are met.

Financing

This is an important aspect of any event; it is often forgotten until it becomes obvious that a loss is looming. What is the source of income? Is the competition to be sponsored or self-financing, or a bit of each? What is the spending limit? What income can be generated from entry fees, programmes, ticket sales, sponsors, sales of goods at the event, etc.?

Make out an estimated expenditure sheet to cover the hire of the hall, printing (tickets, publicity and programmes), travelling expenses for officials, lunches for officials and competitors, buffet afterwards, possibly a disco, and trophies. Take this to the organising committee for approval. Aim to make a profit, or at worst to break even. If there are sponsors, make sure you know the conditions under which they are offering support. Sponsors are not just giving money away: they expect a return. If they get a good return they will probably support you again in the future.

Booking the hall

You will probably be using a school hall or a public hall at a sports centre. Ascertain the charge, and make sure that you have it in writing. Check out all the possible extras. Carrying on beyond the time stated may cost you a great deal, as may additional services from the hirer. Confirm the booking in writing and get your deposit in in time.

Publicity

If you want spectators, you must organise publicity for the event. Posters will be necessary. They should be of size A4 or, better, A3, and printed in one colour on a plain background for economy. Check the prices and find out the cost for larger amounts: having twice as many copies will increase the price only slightly. Get an attractive design if you can: good posters can be sold at the competition. A5 or A4 sheets can easily be sent around with ticket order-forms.

Remember that early sales are money in the bank. A good audience can bring in a large amount of money, if the tickets are realistically priced, and generate a good atmosphere.

Contact all thc nearby schools, radio stations and newspapers well before the event and draw attention to any local or star performers. Competition alone makes the event interesting. Try to avoid dates when there are other important local happenings.

Entries

Produce an entry form which clearly indicates the cost and conditions of entry, the date and time of the competition, the closing date for entry and any conditions of late entry. Additional information may include directions, refund conditions, insurance conditions and, most important, the routines for the competition. The cost of entry must be realistic: the value of the prizes will help your calculation of it.

Officials

Many officials are needed to run a competition, and they should be contacted well beforehand. Remember that you should have qualified judges: get a list from the local BTF divisional secretary. Confirm their availability in writing.

You will need, depending on the size of the competition and the number of age groups or categories, superior judges, assistant superior judges, judges for form, difficulty judges, scribes for the judges, recorders for the scores, runners and score displayers, spotters, an arena manager, competitors' stewards, general helpers, an announcer, programme sellers, catering helpers, and typists or mini-computer operators equipped with duplicators and/or photocopiers for the scores.

Make sure that you have sent written invitations to any local officials who may have given permission, important guests from the sponsors and the local committee for the sport, and the press. See that you have someone to meet them all, and have easily accessible seats reserved for them. Provide teas or refreshments at the interval or afterwards. Invite the competitors to the post-competition party, if you have one: the guests may want to meet the performers.

Setting out

Have a plan of the arena. Work out beforehand where everything is to be set out—trampolines, crash mats, judges, scorers, competitors' seats, presentation podium and trophies. (Do not leave the trophies out all day: some may disappear.)

Remember that the judges are to sit on raised seats 1m (3¼ft) and 5m (16½ft) from the trampolines (rule 23.1). In many halls this can cause problems.

If there are to be invited guests, it may be necessary to seat them on special seats within the confines of the arena. If there is to be a televised recording or broadcast of the event, the power sources must be found and the entrances checked to see if the equipment can be brought in. If there is to be computer scoring, small power sources are needed. The public-address system for the announcer needs to be checked for efficiency—a muffled sound from the speakers can make the whole information service a problem. A photocopier or duplicator for results is necessary; make sure you have enough paper.

DURING THE COMPETITION

If all the arrangements have been made efficiently, the competition should run easily.

The superior judge is in charge of the running of the competition and should see that it goes through without delay. An extra five or ten seconds added onto the time for each competitor can add up to a considerable over-run at the end of a competition with a couple of hundred routines.

Make sure that the competitors' steward is well informed in advance of everything that he or she is expected to do. This should avoid delays in getting the stream of competitors onto the trampoline.

Make sure that the competitors are kept in the competitors' enclosure and not allowed to wander about the audience or arena too freely, giving the impression of disorder. The announcer should be briefed to announce the next item on the programme frequently, so that any competitors who have moved out of the arena can be brought back in good time for their event or round.

Presentations

The presentation should be well organised so that the final part of the event rounds off a good day's competition. Book someone to present the awards—you may wish to honour more than one person. Make sure that you have asked them, preferably in writing, well before the event, indicating what age group or groups you would like them for. If there is a sponsor, ask a representative of the company to make a presentation.

With regard to speeches, you may have to put up with some long-winded ones. Try to get your best speaker along to say a public thank-you to those who have had a part to play—the mayor, the sponsor, the headmaster, the officials, the competitors, the helpers and parents and anyone else involved. It is good policy to thank the organiser, since that job starts well before the event and continues well after.

Immediately after the presentation, the announcer should work to get the participants out of the arena so that the clearing-up can begin.

AFTER THE COMPETITION

You should prepare your work-force before the competition starts. If you have not done this, you may find that you are left to clear up while everyone else goes off to celebrate. Use reliable people, and get the job done quickly. It is normally much easier to take everything apart than it was to put it together. Have plenty of receptacles for the rubbish. Leave the place as you found it—you may wish to return.

Thanks

One of the most important jobs after the competition is writing the thank-you letters. Everyone who assisted should receive one. This may take time, but then so did helping at the competition. At the very least you should send a duplicated letter. Make sure that people who gave money or services in quantity get a letter mentioning the part they played: they may wish to show this to their own superiors. The manager of the sports centre may find it useful if you write mentioning the service given by the staff.

Final financial winding-up

Pay the bills promptly. Collect all the cheques and cash and bank them, having made a complete record. Get receipts for any cash payments you make, or you may forget to whom you made them. It is always wise to pay from a float rather than from the receipts, keeping the two separate. Make sure that you get bills and claims for expenses in writing. Try to finalise everything within about a week, so that confusion is not created as memory fades.

Debriefing

It is often very useful to get the main organising committee together two or three weeks after the event to run through the successes and failures of the competition. This will help to make the next one better.

Appendix 2

The BTF proficiency scheme

Using the scheme

The proficiency scheme developed by the BTF has been graded to give any teacher or coach a progressive way to take a pupil from the very beginnings of jumping to a very advanced state. There are progressions for all the difficult moves, and each grade has, as optional, moves which are compulsory in the next grade. In addition, it supplies a series of routines which will give practice to those who wish to compete.

It is necessary to be a member of the BTF to use the scheme; and, in order to keep up the standards, the awards must be examined by a BTF coach—this also helps ensure that safety is built into the use of the scheme. For a school to use the scheme it must have taken out a membership for the school, and the same applies to sports centres or clubs. (This ruling does not apply to the preliminary award, which is at a very low level and serves to introduce and attract people to the scheme. Anyone can use the preliminary scheme and apply for badges.) League competitions for the number of passes obtained are run, and a cup is given in the London and South-East area for the top club.

Most education authorities demand that those who teach for them are qualified coaches, and so in most schools there is a qualified coach to examine for the awards.

Grades of the scheme

The scheme has ten grades. Starting with the lowest, these are (1) preliminary, (2) elementary bronze, (3) elementary silver, (4) elementary gold, (5) intermediate bronze, (6) intermediate silver, (7) intermediate gold, (8) advanced bronze, (9) advanced silver and (10) advanced gold. The advanced grades (8 – 10) are difficult enough to tax the talents of any performer, while the elementary grades will suit most school work.

The grades of coach also are tied in with the proficiency scheme. Thus at all levels coaching development and proficiency development are correlated.

Details of the proficiency and coaching schemes are supplied to all members in the *BTF Handbook*. Each division of the BTF has a proficiency secretary who will deal with the supply of badges and copies of the scheme. Information about the scheme can also be obtained from the BTF office.

Working the scheme

It is wisest to work through the scheme systematically, so that in the development of your pupils the main progressions are followed. It is not *impossible* to skip sections, but it is foolish to skip moves and to learn advanced skills too early, whatever the temptation: the practice leads to performers who come to a dead end in their development, since they do not have a range of skills necessary to progress to higher levels. Lack of preparation when attempting advanced skills can be dangerous and can in no way be approved by the BTF. Keep to the scheme and progress will be surer.